Library of
Davidson College

Mystics and Militants

By the same author
Educational Strategy for Developing Societies
Planning for Education in Pakistan
Making Peace

Mystics and Militants

A Study of Awareness, Identity and Social Action

ADAM CURLE

TAVISTOCK PUBLICATIONS

First published in Great Britain in 1972
by Tavistock Publications Limited
11 New Fetter Lane, London EC4
Printed in Great Britain in 12 pt Bembo
by Cox and Wyman Ltd,
Fakenham, Norfolk

SBN 422 73900 6
© Adam Curle 1972

Distributed in the USA by
HARPER & ROW PUBLISHERS, INC.
BARNES & NOBLE IMPORT DIVISION

*To Ben Morris
whose friendship and wisdom have so enriched me
for a quarter of a century*

Contents

	Acknowledgements	*page* ix
1	Introduction	1
2	Awareness	13
3	Identity	26
4	Configurations of Awareness and Identity I	34
5	Configurations of Awareness and Identity II	52
6	Changing Awareness Levels	92
7	Makers of Peace and Violence	103
	Notes	110
	Bibliography	112
	Name Index	117
	Subject Index	119

Acknowledgements

I began to work on the outline of this book while on a sabbatical leave from Harvard University spent as a research fellow at the Richardson Institute for Conflict and Peace Research in London. This year of study was supported by a generous grant from the Carnegie Corporation of New York.

I should like again to express my gratitude to these two institutions, which combined to give me the facilities and the resources, intellectual and pecuniary, to write *Making Peace*, to which *Mystics and Militants* constitutes a sort of sequel. Needless to say, nothing I have written in either work represents, save by coincidence, the opinions of anyone associated with either the Carnegie Corporation or the Richardson Institute.

1 Introduction

A few months before beginning to write this book, I completed another entitled *Making Peace* (Curle, 1971). Although I hope that the present work stands on its own, it is, in a sense, a companion volume, concerned with the people in peacemaking situations rather than with the situations themselves or the process of making peace. I should, therefore, begin with a few words about the earlier book.

PEACEMAKING AND UNPEACEFUL RELATIONSHIPS

The previous book dealt, fairly obviously, with peacemaking, but I must first define what I mean by peace.

In the first place, I don't like to use the word by itself. Everyone talks about peace, supposedly loves it, but does little to promote it: often, in fact, the reverse. The term has a vague, idealistic, emotional flavour; it is a word beloved by politicians, preachers, and the mistier sorts of do-gooder. One can, however, bring it down to earth by using it only in the context of *peaceful relationships*. In fact what we mean by peace, if we think of it without getting hung up on the emotion, is that two people, or groups, or nations are getting on well *together*. I shall use peace only in this sense of peaceful relations.

But a peaceful relationship is not simply one in which there is no overt violence: it is one in which there is no conflict. Even more, it is not simply a coexistence that can readily degenerate into strife: it is something more positive – a happy and fruitful partnership, the collaboration of a successful common market, or a congenial marriage.

I should emphasize that conflict and violence are not synonymous, though we often use the words as if they were. By conflict,

I mean a conflict of interests in the sense that, in a given relationship, A's advantage is B's disadvantage. There may well be no violence. The disadvantaged party may even be content, or at least apathetic and accepting, as are many oppressed communities throughout the world. If, however, one examines the condition of such a community, carefully, one discovers much objective evidence of the damaging effects of the conflict. By comparison with the dominating group, the infant mortality rate is higher, average weight and height are lower, literacy is low, there is less political and economic freedom, less occupational mobility, and more police victimization.[1] Moreover, the ruling group owes its affluence and comfort to the cheap labour of the underdogs. Such a relationship cannot be termed peaceful. In the first place, it denies to the members of one group the chance to become what they had it in them to become; and, second, it is very likely, in the long run, to break up in actual violence. For many decades, for example, the black Americans bore their harsh lot with docility, but in the last few years violence has become a significant element in race relations in the USA.

I would underline the point that the damage done to the weaker party in an unpeaceful relationship is not necessarily inflicted by actively harmful measures; it can equally be brought about in a passive way, through failure to do things that could have been done to alleviate distress.[2]

A glance around the world reveals how depressingly many unpeaceful relationships there are. I would not suggest that there are more than there were in the past, but modern news coverage has made it more possible to be aware of them. Many of them are, in addition, on a larger scale, and a number are interlinked.

In *Making Peace* I gave a number of case studies of different types of unpeaceful relationship and then discussed the various peacemaking techniques by which unpeaceful relations can, by stages, be transformed into peaceful ones.

The prototypical unpeaceful relationship is that of a master and slave, where the slave is ignorant of the enormity of his position and of the fact that it could ever be changed, and so apathetically accepts it. This situation can be altered only by what I broadly term *education*, implying some growth of awareness of his position in the slave.

Once the slave (or dominated group) is aware, he (or it) struggles to reach a position of equality with his master (or the ruling group) so that their relationship can be reordered in accordance with principles of justice. This is the stage of confrontation. (Without going into a highly controversial argument, I should simply say that I strongly advocate non-violent techniques of confrontation.)

These two methods, education and confrontation, constitute what might be termed the revolutionary stages of peacemaking, whose primary aim is to reduce the imbalance of power between the parties concerned. They are followed by three processes that are more appropriate to equal than to unequal parties in conflict. By techniques of *conciliation*, hostile individuals are brought to the point where they perceive each other with less unreasonable fear and hostility so that they can, with some hope of success, begin the process of *bargaining* which leads to a settlement of the dispute and a resolution of the conflict. Finally, there is a stage of *development* in which the negative absence of hostilities is transformed into a positive collaboration through an agreement which enables both parties not only to live together without discord but to help each other through appropriate forms of co-operation.

It does not require much insight to realize that the great majority of the world's unpeaceful relationships are between unequal parties and are based on injustice and exploitation. It is true that we appear more immediately menaced by the clash of the great equals, but the volume of suffering caused by the indifference and moral callousness of the advantaged towards the disadvantaged, besides being a disgrace to humanity, is cumulatively just as great a danger and indeed is not dissociated from it.

In *Making Peace* I concentrated on the situations and the peacemaking methods. Only in the conclusions did I tentatively suggest that much depended on the peacemakers themselves. Here the emphasis is on these people, particularly those concerned with the greatly needed revolutionary stages.

In writing about the people who try to change unpeaceful

relationships into peaceful ones (and also about those who try to maintain the unpeaceful ones), I am pursuing two main strands of interest. The first, obviously, is in the whole process of peacemaking. The second is in the remarkable growth of awareness I have noticed throughout the world – especially among the young, but also among their parents – of injustice, inhumanity, oppression, and victimization. It is these 'aware' people who are committed to attempting to make the social changes that I consider to be an intrinsic part of the progression of peacemaking. What are they like? What motivates them? What difficulties do they encounter? Who are those who stand in their way? The bulk of the book is taken up with these issues, but I should perhaps first try to answer the questions: How do they see the world? What is it that they oppose?

THE EXPLOITATIVE NETWORK

I apply this term to a worldwide situation which enables the rich and privileged to establish and maintain power over the poor and underprivileged and which, I believe, has deeply influenced the thinking of militant youth.

It can perhaps be most clearly recognized in the relations between the rich and the poor nations. The former exercise an extraordinary degree of economic and political (the two are obviously closely related) control over most nations of the Third World. They buy raw materials cheaply from them and sell back products manufactured from these same materials at a high price. In order to exercise this domination the wealthy nations have to make allies of certain elites in the Third World who are prepared, for personal or political profit, to collaborate with them in what Pierre Jalée terms the pillage of the Third World (Jalée, 1968). Just as the rich nations despoil the poor ones, so the richer classes and regions (particularly the towns) in the poor nations despoil the already impoverished classes and areas (particularly the rural zones). Just as the terms of trade are bad, on the international scale, for the Third World *vis-à-vis* the rich countries, so they are within the Third World between town and country. Although no one would claim that the rich nations are acting in concert – indeed, they are in competition with each other – pricing policies are established which in general favour the economies of the rich countries rather than the poor.

Thus there is, in a sense, a worldwide system of exploitation of the poor by the rich, a vast network of unpeaceful relationships occasioned by the rapacity of the rich. The pockets of poverty within such giants of wealth as the USA, and the failure of several Labour governments, according to Titmuss (1962) and others (Blackburn & Cockburn, 1967), to reduce the inequalities in Great Britain, must be seen as part of this network.

I must stress that I am referring not only to such flagrant examples of neo-imperialist control as exist in several Latin American states, but to the very large number of nations in Africa and Asia which have been forced to abandon a considerable measure of autonomy in return for economic advantages which only make them more completely the pawns of the rich donors of loans and other forms of assistance.[3] The Tanzanias are few and far between.[4]

This same network sustains the relationship between the black and white peoples of South Africa. The whites are supported, despite occasional sanctimonious admonitions about their policy of apartheid, by the wealthy nations who gain much advantage from the association.

The great majority of these relationships are not violent ones, even if we take into account guerrilla warfare in perhaps half the Latin American nations and in southern Africa. The existence of actual war, or prolonged and massive mutual violence, implies some degree of balance of power.[5] (I judge this to some extent empirically. The USA is clearly stronger in many respects than the NLF–North Vietnam combination, but in several years of struggle neither has been able to defeat the other. I therefore posit that in the context of the war in Southeast Asia there is a considerable similarity in the total potency of the contestants although it is manifested in different ways: the Americans have the manpower and the equipment, their enemies have the morale and the skill in jungle fighting.) Clearly, wars may originate in disagreements between more or less equivalent powers – the India/Pakistan war of

1965 comes to mind – which have nothing to do with the network of exploitation. When two approximately balanced groups have a dispute, the restoration of a peaceful relationship depends on the conventional techniques of conflict resolution – conciliation, mediation, and bargaining – rather than on eradicating injustices and inequalities. Nevertheless, wars such as those in Vietnam and in the Middle East are closely related to the interests of the rich nations: although their resolution depends largely upon a local accommodation, it must also be one that will satisfy the rich.

The strength, ubiquity, and complexity of the exploitative network are such that those who wish to promote peace (as I define it) cannot but feel daunted. What is needed, they may well believe, is not simply an attack on a specific injustice, a wrong righted here, a good cause espoused there, but a wholesale change in the structure of a society in which established authority holds the trump cards. It is all too easy to listen to the blandishments of those in power who would say: 'But of course we want the same as you. We don't want unrest – it's bad for business. We don't want inequality either, because it leads to unrest. Our interests coincide and we must learn to help each other.' But clever rulers have always been adept at handing out soporifics – amiable words and minor concessions which confuse or conceal the real nature of the conflicts and thereby achieve political quiescence.

COMPETITIVE MATERIALISM

The psychological corollary of the exploitative network, its great stay and support, is competitive materialism. This is as old as man, has roots that invade the centre of his being, and is also at the base, as we shall see later, of what I term belonging-identity, an attitude that does much to prevent social change.

Competitive materialism is not only the corollary to, but also the psychic background of, the exploitative network because it upholds the external measure by which success (and so, often, virtue) can be assessed. In rich societies the criterion for success is riches: one becomes wealthy through individualist striving after material gain. No matter if one's competitors are crushed; that is part of the implacable game of getting on top.

Today, this phenomenon has been given fresh impetus, and a frightening new hold over us, through the advent of advanced technology. To the ancient rapacity and cunning greed have been added cool disengaged analysis, the passionless experiment, and the meticulous material objectivity through which technical advances are made. To the old empiricism and pragmatism (what brought profit was what worked) is added a scorn for what is not quantifiable or measurable. The technological quantum jump has, among other things, greatly facilitated the operations of the exploitative network. The more we develop, the less we need the Third World's materials, and the more ingeniously we process and employ what we do need for further technological processes.

I am not, unlike some writers in this field such as Roszak (1967), against materialism as an approach to phenomena. I am far from despising science, and science cannot flourish without experiment and objectivity. But when it is allied to a competitive and individualistic ethos, it becomes all pervasive, expanding into areas that pertain more appropriately to imagination and fantasy, to the unconscious rather than the conscious, the twilight rather than the blaze of day. Moreover, it is technology – the technique of doing things – rather than science – the art of understanding things – that prevails. Technology is based on science, it is true, but it can debase scientific findings if, in its supremacy, it employs science for debased tasks.

When the younger generations protest against materialism, they are referring not only to the ravenously exclusive pursuit of wealth, possessions, and position, but to an attitude of mind – serving this goal – which diminishes the role of imagination, the artistic, the subjective, the mystical. It is an attitude of mind that seems to them to be anti-human, producing a society in which the full development of human beings as creatures that feel as well as cerebrate is impaired. Its most malignant quality, indeed, is that it captures the minds of those who, when younger, opposed it. So persuasive is its capacity to call into existence needs which it alone can satisfy, that a man must be particularly strong and aware to remain outside the system and not be drawn into the exploitative network, for the two are interlocking.

The alliance between the exploitative network and competitive materialism has produced two other great dangers that menace mankind – pollution and nuclear war.

It is not necessary to expand much on these. Pollution results from the greedy, acquisitive, selfish use of technology to produce goods at minimum expense to the owners of the means of production. Hence, the carelessly callous disposal of waste-products in river, sea, and atmosphere. Hence the reckless use of insecticides.

Nuclear war, made possible by scientific and technological expertise, is made probable by the policies of those who possess the weapons. Clearly the circumstances that could lead to a nuclear war are both complex and variable. In this context I need only say that, whatever the circumstances, they are built on a substratum of self-interest. Those who have great possessions take extreme measures to protect them. These measures may become an effective part of the system. In the United States, for example, the relationship between industry and the military has become one of symbiosis. Competitive materialism operating the exploitative network has built up interests to defend, while the construction of a means of defence has created more riches, that is more interests requiring more defence, and so it goes on. It is hard not to feel that the expansion of the means of defence (which could more simply be termed the means of destruction) has developed an autonomous momentum. Disarmament is agonizingly hard to achieve, whereas nothing is easier than to speed up an arms race.

AWARENESS AND IDENTITY

In attempting to discover how men and women respond to the perception of the world I have just outlined – and I believe this perception to be commonly held by at least the younger generation – I fall back on concepts of identity and awareness that were delineated briefly in *Making Peace*. In that book I was interested in the way which people in critical conflict situations changed their attitudes both to their enemies and to themselves. They tended to become extreme to the point of irrationality in these attitudes. Their foes were without exception sinister, evil, and determined on destruction; they, by contrast, were of almost knightly virtue. Thus it appeared to me that their *awareness* of both themselves and their situation diminished sharply. At the same time, they built up a new sense of *identity* based on their own courage and patriotism and reinforced by contrast with the wickedness of the enemy.

I became increasingly convinced that the interrelations of different levels of awareness and identity could provide us with clues to the understanding of many aspects of human behaviour, particularly in regard to social action. Looking further, I saw that there were different modes of both awareness and identity and that these combined in configurations which had quite specific implications for how people saw and reacted to the problems of society.

Awareness, meaning essentially self-awareness and hence insight into the conditions of others, can be higher or lower. Identity can be either a sense of knowing who one is, based upon awareness (that is, awareness-identity), or, what is more usual, a sense of belonging (that is, belonging-identity), and both of these can be stronger or weaker. When the belonging mode of identity predominates, we define ourselves in terms of what we belong to or what belongs to us, whether it be a civilization or cultural tradition, family or country, material possessions or social position, professional achievements or tastes in music, or any combination of these or innumerable other things.

The greater part of this book is taken up with describing the various modes of awareness and identity, and the effects of different combinations of them – that is, high and low awareness coupled with strong and weak identity in its belonging and awareness forms.

Broadly speaking, the combination of low awareness and a strong belonging-identity produces the conservative, stabilizing force in society. People in this category find their identity in belonging, therefore they tend to want to keep things as they are, sometimes to the extent of preserving what they know intellectually to be wrong. Alternatively, or additionally, they strengthen their sense of belonging through acquisitiveness. (There are other behaviour patterns in this configuration, but they need not concern us now.)

The militants and mystics who provide the title of this book are those who have sufficient awareness to perceive the objective necessity to change dehumanizing circumstances for the better, coupled with a weak belonging-identity which does not tie them to the *status quo*. They are divided into these two groups according to their prevailing mode of awareness. I describe awareness as *natural*, which speaks for itself; or *self-conscious*, when it derives from purposive efforts to widen consciousness through psychotherapy or sensitivity training or something similar; or *supraliminal*, when an attempt is made to achieve some sort of mystical or religious insight. The militants are mostly people of natural or self-conscious awareness. In people who are exceptionally aware, such as Gandhi, the militant and the mystic mode tend to merge, but at the level with which most of us are concerned the militants provide the active role in society, attempting to change institutions they deem to be bad, while the mystics, whatever their ultimate goals, are more preoccupied with changing themselves. If I were to make a crude typification, I would class the New Left and the Students for Democratic Society as militants, and the hippies in general with perhaps the Beatles in particular as mystics.

Only in the last chapter shall I specifically return to what I term the peacemaking roles of militants and mystics. Until that point I am engaged in defining the types. Nevertheless a considerable amount is said in passing, and even more can be inferred, about the relationship of these types to revolutionary social change.

SOURCES AND AUTHORITY

It is a good thing to let the reader know what sort of book he is starting to read. He may approach it, otherwise, with false expectations, being resentful if it does not turn out as he expected, and comparing it unfavourably with books of the type to which he expected it would conform. I would first make it clear that what follows does not result from experimental studies or from any work that could be quantified. It is based on what I have myself done and seen. Readers of *Making Peace* will know something about this, since my experience forms the basis of illustrative case studies, but I will give a brief summary here.

Since the end of the Second World War I have been considerably involved with students, both militants and mystics, in England and Europe, in the USA, in several parts of Africa, and in Pakistan. I have known the suffering of men opposing obnoxious policies. In addition to having acted in a mediatory capacity in two violent international conflicts, I have been involved in a wide range of unpeaceful situations including industrial disputes, racial conflicts in Africa and the USA, tribal clashes, palace revolutions, and unjust and oppressive tyrannies in remote parts of the world. I have been concerned with development in about twenty countries in the Middle East, North and sub-Saharan Africa, Latin America and the Caribbean, and Asia. In the course of all this I have had many enlightening experiences, including confrontations with the authorities in several countries. I have twice been captured by men planning to kill me, and on numerous occasions I have been hungry, ill, or lost in wild mountain country or desert. Over this period I have met many wise men and learnt what I could from them. During the last few years, which have been particularly poignant for me, I have been very close to a gigantic tragedy in which hundreds of thousands died for nothing. I have also been in a position to be very close to a group of the most aware young people in the world, students at Harvard University. I mention all this only to suggest that I am not speaking abstractly of people (including myself) in strange or extreme situations.

I admit readily that I lack most of the tools of psychological analysis. I have not trained as an analyst and cannot pretend to share the insights of those who are practised in any branch of depth psychology. I feel diffident in using the concept of identity elaborated with such richness by Erikson, a psychoanalyst of genius. My qualifications for treating of this type of material are, first, I suppose, that I have in fact been dealing with it constantly at an unprofessional level in the course of my life and have time and again been concerned with issues of what I call identity and awareness or mask and mirage, with mystics and militants, with people steeped in belonging-identity. Professionally, I have had the inestimable advantage of having been an early staff member of the Tavistock Institute of Human Relations; while my competence to discuss psychological topics might also be thought to be validated by my having written my doctoral thesis largely about an aspect of group therapy, and having held two university appointments in psychology as well as two in other fields. (I should perhaps admit that such qualifications mean little to me: if a man can do something, he can; if he can't, nothing in his curriculum vitae makes much difference.)

My last relevant attribute is that I know something of Oriental religions and psycho-philosophical systems.

When I began to write I tried to find a justification for every tentative conclusion by referring to the works of others, but quickly abandoned this attempt. I was beginning to construct a system for which I and my experience had to bear the responsibility: I could not blame it on others.

But no man stands alone intellectually. He is immeasurably indebted to both predecessors and contemporaries. I would be nowhere without W. R. Bion and Ronald Fairbairn, Eric Trist and Ben Morris, without Sigmund Freud and Melanie Klein and Erik Erikson, without Ronald Laing, Abraham Maslow, Erich Fromm, and Norman O. Brown, without Ouspensky, Gurdjieff, Suzuki, and Evans-Wentz.[6] These and many others have supplied the shafts of insight which I have perhaps misapplied or misconstrued in building my system. I thank them and beg their pardon for the possible abuse of their ideas. I only affirm that they cannot be held accountable for the totality I have attempted to construct.

2 Awareness

Since a concept of awareness is crucial to my theme, I must define it with care. In my terms, there are both levels and types of awareness: we may be more, or less, aware, and the awareness we possess may be of different sorts which are to some extent but not wholly determined by their level. Awareness essentially means self-awareness, a man's consciousness of his own being. However, what we perceive about the inner world determines what we perceive about the outer. If our self-perceptions are dull or distorted, it is unlikely that we will perceive others clearly and accurately. If we can empathize with our friends it is improbable that we will experience extreme guilt and irrational self-loathing.

(Here I should interpolate a definition within a definition. I have just used the word irrational and shall use it and its synonyms again. But to refer to something as irrational or rational implies the existence of a standard of what is more or less correct. How can there be such a standard when something so nebulous and indefinable is involved as states of mind? In order to avoid getting hung up on what could become an intricate discussion I employ the simple expedient of consensus. If a man sees himself very differently from how his friends see him, then, provided his friends are normal common-sensical persons, I would suspect him of a measure of irrationality. I would further suspect that his view of his friends would differ in significant respects from their assessment of themselves and of each other. Thus rationality and awareness are related, converging from time to time to identicality, then separating.)

Perhaps the best way to approach the concept of awareness is to start with states of low awareness. These are conditions, experienced frequently by virtually everyone and by some for a great part of their lives, in which people have little understanding of their motives, their actions, or the sources of their feelings. In a state of low awareness we act and speak relatively automatically, *without in the fullest sense knowing what we are doing*. Changing moods flicker across the screen of consciousness – worry, self-satisfaction, irritation – following some erratic and hidden sequence of emotional discharges. We do or say things we subsequently regret and observe shamefacedly, 'I don't know what came over me' or 'I didn't think'. We talk without listening to ourselves, turning on the record appropriate to the occasion, as it were, and letting it speak for us. Above all, we are not self-consciously aware of our own identity. When we are operating at a low level of awareness it is as though we have switched to the automatic pilot and gone to sleep. But the automatic pilot may lead us in a direction we would not have taken had we been awake.

To be unaware also means to live on the surface, to ignore what lies below the top level of consciousness, to neglect the instinctive or intuitive aspect of personality, to lead a flat two-dimensional psychic life. But, of course, to deny awareness of the inner life does not make it go away. It means, paradoxically, that we are the more likely to be dominated by it. The monstrous fears, the guilt, the shameful longings, the celestial visions, the viper, the baboon, and the angel which comprise our inner pantheon make us, through their interrelations, what we are. To be unaware is to deny our essence. Essence denied turns sour. If we do not act out what we are, we cease to be it. The darker and the frightening sides of our potential become more dominant, because we are not fully aware of them. If we recognized them for what they were, they would, contradictorily, change their nature. But since we sense them obscurely, not as elements to be assessed, appreciated, and incorporated into awareness but as phantasms, grotesque and horrifying, we turn aside, fearing to look more closely. But they are there, the rulers of our being, dictating every mood, every emotional need, every irrational fear and compulsive action. Thus to be unaware also means to be unfree, to lack autonomy, because we have no conscious control over the factors that are driving us. Conversely, if we did possess awareness, not only would we be better able to order our actions, physical and psychic, but the determining factors would themselves be different. The essence would no longer be sour. The purpose of most psychotherapy is precisely to restore this type of autonomy.[7]

It is possible to confuse unawareness with spontaneity. The argument goes as follows. Spontaneous people are straightforward and natural; spontaneity is a pure, unstudied, even instinctual response to a situation; it is therefore a good thing. If awareness (as opposed to this idea of unawareness) involves a more studied and careful response, a regrettable loss of spontaneity will also result. Unawareness, therefore, promotes spontaneity and is desirable. I have frequently heard this line of reasoning and think that it includes several errors. First, the apparently spontaneous response made in a state of low awareness may be little more than an automatic reflex, possibly highly inappropriate and to be regretted later. Second, the response may not even appear to be spontaneous. It may be laboured and confused. It may, in fact, be an elaborately thought-out response, except that vital internal factors have not been taken into account in framing it. Moreover, though awareness may promote deliberation, it also fosters what I term true spontaneity. By this I mean that people who have access to the essential parts of their make-up are able to respond swiftly and positively. True spontaneity can be recognized by its warmth. The automatic spontaneity of unawareness may equally well be cruel, violent, or selfish.

It is all too simple to consider unawareness in extreme terms. The obsessional neurotic, the drunkard, the man in what is significantly termed 'a blind rage', are all obvious examples of people who are both, and for the same reason, out of touch with and out of control of themselves. But I am not concerned here with pathological exaggerations. They may be useful caricatures to drive points home, but this book is essentially about 'average', 'normal', or 'healthy' human beings. I have no ambition to show that highly disturbed people lead impoverished lives or bring grief and confusion to their associates. This we already know. What we fail to recognize so clearly is the effect upon our lives and society of the very common, very *usual* modes of mental functioning, such as low levels of awareness. Most of us are relatively unaware a great deal of the time. We do not actually accept this, for to do so would imply an incompatible degree of awareness of ourselves. We quite simply consider our mental processes, if indeed we consider them at all, to be perfectly all right, to be natural. I shall try, however, to show that our concept of naturalness carries the seeds of our destruction.

Levels of awareness change. We fluctuate, for reasons that are discussed later, from higher to lower awareness. Moments of reflective self-consciousness are chased away by nebulous anxieties, threats to self-esteem, or the desire to show off, only to steal back again when the more negative emotion has purged itself. Our lack of complete awareness and control is demonstrated by the fact that these changes occur unobserved by the person in whom they are happening. When he shifts to a lower level of awareness, he forgets the person he was just before at a higher level of awareness.

Although levels of awareness move constantly up and down, people have a centre of gravity, an average level that is higher or lower. Why this should be so is not clear. Much depends, no doubt, on heredity, and on the accident of early environment. I am inclined also to believe that a man's values and moral code are significant. A most important factor is a felt need to raise the level of awareness. This may lead a person to undergo some form of depth psychotherapy when unawareness is having obviously painful consequences, or to practise some form of mental discipline aimed at widening his consciousness. It is undoubtedly true that many young people have recourse to drugs for the same reason, but while drugs may, or may appear to, expand consciousness, they do not, in my terms, raise the level of a man's awareness of himself. Certainly they do not confer that increased autonomy which is a corollary of awareness.

It is easier to describe the lower levels of awareness than the higher ones. The simplest reason for this is that while we all have direct experience of the former, we know the highest levels only by inference. We know that certain people have had profound insight into human existence and the natural world, and we have read the literature or seen and heard the works of art in which they expressed their awareness. But this does not tell us what it was to be them, or the nature of the experiences at such a level of awareness. Pascal, attempting to describe his mystical feelings, used the one word *feu*.[8] If someone tells us that he has known fear or rage, we know what he means because we have also. But *fire*? Thus, although we have all experienced levels of awareness that were considerably higher than our lowest ones, we cannot, unless we claim to share the awareness of a Jesus, Socrates, Shakespeare, Rembrandt, Bach, Leonardo, Buddha, Gandhi, Milaepa, or Gurdjieff, comprehend the ceiling – or indeed know if there is a ceiling. For this reason, I proceed cautiously with my description of three types of awareness, mostly at higher levels.

NATURAL AWARENESS

One may possess a considerable amount of awareness without having been psychoanalysed or joined a mystical cult, or in any other way probed one's psyche. I call this natural awareness.

A man whose centre of balance is at a reasonably high level of natural awareness, and I know many, has several recognizable qualities. He has a balanced view of himself. He does not, as is frequent at lower levels, alternate between self-glorification and self-abuse (an interesting word). Instead, he sees himself as others see him, a man with certain capacities and positive qualities, and certain failings and follies. He does not, however, torment himself about his inadequacies, or puff himself up about his abilities. He tries sensibly, but without desperation, to improve his skills and to overcome his defects. If he is a religious man, he prays, but in any case, religious or not, he uses common sense to create conditions in which he can do better and avoid upsetting mistakes. He is definite about himself, but at the same time somewhat detached and compassionate about his own nature. Claiming responsibility for neither virtues nor vices, he can afford to be relaxed in carrying out what is his responsibility – the strengthening of the former and the weakening of the latter.

When we are at this level of awareness, we are likely to behave as reasonably and as positively towards others as we do towards ourselves. At lower levels, we are more apt to exploit others in order to assuage the anxious self-doubt created by our unacknowledged selves. Because we are only half-aware, and so feel anxious and inadequate, we seek confirmation of our potency or realness, or punishment for our sins, by dominating or being dominated. In countless ways we manipulate others to obtain relief from the pains of unawareness. But a higher level of awareness renders this unnecessary. People are met in their own right rather than as potential threats or supports to another individual's tender psyche.

A certain objectivity is perhaps the keynote of this type of awareness – about oneself, about others, and hence about values. One way of defining objectivity is to say that emotions do not interfere with perceptions. If this is true of the relationships between a man and his fellows, it also applies to the moral system in the light of which he regulates those relationships. The moral values of unawareness are more apt to be subjective and selfish, those of higher awareness to be objective and altruistic.

It is important to guard against the danger of becoming excessively interested in awareness, too wrapped up in the examination of our motives, sensations, and behaviour. Such a concentration of the specifics of thought or action may easily preclude an unforced total sense of self, which I take to be the essence of awareness. Paradoxically, we may lose awareness by achieving it to a limited extent, which reveals the parts rather than the whole, or by wrong methods, by which I mean seeking awareness as a gratification rather than because without it we are incomplete. A further paradox is that the higher our level of awareness the less we concentrate upon it, having dissolved many of the quirks, the fears and shames, the wants and ambitions, which comprised our personality. What remains is not the ego as we had perceived it, but a capacity for relating to others (awareness of them) unvitiated by the demands of the ego.

SELF-CONSCIOUS AWARENESS

I use this term specifically for awareness derived from contrived experiences aimed at revealing the source of motives, attitudes, values, and behaviour patterns. Such experiences would include psychoanalysis and other forms of psychotherapy, T-groups, sensitivity training, and the like. One objective of these techniques is to widen a consciousness which has been circumscribed by pathological factors (such as neurosis) or by conventional habits of expressing, or not expressing, feelings. They claim to reveal and develop what is hidden, stunted, disconnected.

Natural and self-conscious awareness are not mutually incompatible or inconsistent. They can certainly be employed to support each other. A man with a good level of natural awareness may be helped to further understanding by analytic insights, while an analysand who has high natural awareness will respond more readily than one who has not.

Ideally, self-conscious awareness will reach greater heights than natural awareness. Its systematic and purposeful probing will reveal more than do the fortuitous circumstances of natural awareness. There are, however, two potentially adverse circumstances. Depth psychology may be associated with somewhat dogmatic systems which are initially essential for arranging information and ideas, but may end by imposing a stifling or obfuscating orthodoxy. As in the case of religious belief, it demands a great man to get behind the official creed to the core of truth it aims to protect, but finally merely conceals. The second disadvantage is that the experience of therapy or training may engender a degree of self-absorption that impedes the growth of relaxed and objective relationships with others.

SUPRALIMINAL AWARENESS

This form of awareness is the hardest to describe and the one most readily counterfeited. It results, in my definition, from specific efforts to expand consciousness, to achieve a different type of perception. Thus it differs from the other sorts of awareness where a raising of the level means an improvement but not a change in the kind of vision. Supraliminal awareness is mystical and religious; the others are secular and practical. Supraliminal awareness is directed towards such goals as the purification of the soul, the achievement of inner unity, samadhi, union with God, the ecstatic vision, nirvana, the annihilation of the personality, the achievement of Buddhahood, and so on (some of these goals are incompatible). Higher levels of natural and self-conscious awareness are directed towards such goals as the improvement of social relations, the bringing about of social change, the promotion of mental health.

But we must distinguish between what men strive for and the awareness they actually experience. Many people are drawn to the idea of supraliminal awareness because it offers an alternative to competitive materialism. Having sufficient natural or self-conscious awareness to see the world with some clarity, and by the same token to know how little they can affect it, they withdraw from the mainstream and seek a quiet tributary. Most of them would argue, however, that in so doing they are not simply opting out irresponsibly, but actually taking the most positive form of action. How can they reform society unless they first reform themselves? They are withdrawing in order to return as more potent social forces. But it is really hard for us to say how far the acceptance of a social philosophy (that of the counter-culture, for example) coupled with attempts to expand awareness (through recitation of mantras, yoga, transcendental meditation, or drugs), in fact affects awareness. Does perception become more penetrating, more comprehensive, more lucid? Does the relationship between the one and the many become more vivid? Are new truths and greater beauty revealed? And do people, as a result, act in wiser, more harmonious, and more compassionate ways? Or does perception, if indeed it changes at all, serve to seal the individual off from his fellows in a world of fantasy, sometimes beautiful, sometimes horrific? In cases where awareness has reached new levels, it is difficult to communicate the changes in perception except through the symbolism of art, and it may be that many who have achieved an expansion of awareness are incapable of expressing what it means to them. They will say, for example, that their sense of colour and design is clearer, that they feel their place in the cosmos, that they sense time differently, that they have a feeling for the unity of life. However, unless we have had similar experiences, these are just so many words. They are the expression of what may have been an overpowering and extraordinary revelation, but we do not know what they mean and the impression they make upon us is either banal or sentimental.

To confuse the issue, the visions of mystics frequently resemble the visions of psychotics. Does this mean that the mystics are mad or that the insane have flashes of greater insight than the sane? Both, perhaps, can on occasion be true, but to pursue the matter further would lead into a semantic morass which is irrelevant to the theme of this book. I believe that it is by its fruits rather than by the visions it claims that awareness is to be recognized. If greater sensitivity and a livelier compassion are accompanied by changes in consciousness, I should conclude that the latter form part of a genuine growth of awareness. I could also conceive that this experience might place great strain on the individual, as must any departure from normality, and that he might on occasion exhibit signs of tension. He would still, however, behave very differently from a man whose unusual perceptions arose out of pathological rather than developmental abnormalities.

I should refer to drugs in this connection. It cannot be denied that they may confer the same type of experience – instant awareness, as it has been termed – as the long-drawn-out practice of spiritual exercises. It seems that some people have achieved a level of awareness through drugs which has profoundly affected their lives. I know, for example, of habitual criminals who, after one dose of LSD, have attained an entirely new perception of themselves and have, as a result, reformed their lives and given up crime. At the same time, there are probably many more for whom the drug experience has become a substitute for existence, dulling awareness of both self and others. There is undoubtedly a chemistry of awareness, for every perceptual change has its neural concomitants, and various drugs affect it, but our knowledge in this field is inadequate. It would seem, however, that uncontrolled and prolonged use of drugs tends to lower rather than to raise awareness.

Lastly, there may be many people whose attempts to gain supraliminal awareness result in no apparent changes in perception. They may intone *om*, meditate cross-legged, fast, do breathing exercises, attach themselves to gurus, study the scriptures, model their lives on saints and holy men – but nothing happens. From our point of view, however, the important thing is that they, like their more successful brethren, have chosen this particular way, the attempt to achieve this type of awareness, as their response to the conditions of the world. This brings us to the crucial issue of the relationship between the different types of awareness, their similarities and their differences.

RELATIONS BETWEEN TYPES OF AWARENESS

Natural awareness we all possess in some degree. Self-conscious awareness we acquire as the result of a particular course of action, such as undergoing therapy. Supraliminal awareness is usually striven for and may or may not be obtained; indeed, we may achieve only a false vision which lowers awareness.

Sometimes, however, it is difficult to distinguish between these modes of awareness. A man with a reasonably high centre of gravity of natural awareness, but with no pretensions to anything more, may have flashes of revelation which completely transcend the normal bounds of consciousness. Insight thus gained when harnessed to technique may be the basis of all great art. How can we tell whether it is a normal extension of the natural or a perception of a quite different order? I tend to maintain that any achievement of man is by definition natural: we do not know the limits of our capacity.

The systems followed in order to achieve awareness further complicate the definitions. It would seem to me that Freudian psychoanalysis clearly heightens natural awareness and, since it is undertaken both purposefully and systematically, it properly falls into the category of promoting self-conscious awareness. But what of Jungian analytical psychology? Here I would say that mystical and Oriental undercurrents coupled with concepts like the collective unconscious tend to move its results more in the direction of supraliminal awareness. Then what about the systems of Ouspensky and Gurdjieff? Though highly esoteric and hence supraliminal in their implications, they are also highly organized methods of revealing the structure of the psyche (though the structure revealed is very different from that perceived by Freud).

For these reasons, supraliminal awareness should be considered less in terms of its content – which it is in any case hard to be sure of – than in terms of what is done in the attempt to achieve it and what it is hoped to get from it. It is in this sense that it should be understood in this book.

In later pages we discuss the ways in which the different levels or types of awareness affect social action. At this point I will simply say that when a person of a reasonable level of natural awareness (high enough, that is, to be aware of the nature of the surrounding society) chooses to seek supraliminal awareness, he is making a particular sort of response to the challenge of his times. At best, he engages in a purposeful effort at self-development with the ultimate object of applying himself to the transformation of society. At worst, he withdraws, adopting a schizoid position in which his awareness diminishes. By contrast, the person who remains naturally or self-consciously aware is more likely to be openly and directly involved in social affairs. He is an activist rather than a dreamer. The choice of the different paths is no doubt governed by deep-seated personality factors: I suggest their analysis as a good Ph.D. thesis topic. But at the highest level the ways meet. Men like Gandhi have been both militant and mystical.

MASK AND MIRAGE

I include in this chapter a discussion of what I call the mask–mirage mechanism, because it is closely associated with questions of awareness.

It is axiomatic that what goes on within us affects our perceptions, not only of ourselves, but of others. The anxieties associated with a low level of awareness spring from hidden fears and guilt about our lust, violence, and general wickedness, in fact about the incompleteness and disunity of our nature. Rather than acknowledge these things we dissociate ourselves from them by the well-tried psychic trick of projection. It is not we who are bad; it is those people. We are good, brave, unselfish, loyal, and pure, and we have, above all, an inner harmony, a real I. They are lewd, mischievous, untrustworthy, lubricious, and demoniacal.

The mechanism by which we both get rid of our own badness (by displacing it onto others) and reassure ourselves of our goodness, I call the mask and mirage technique. The mask is the disguise we put on to fool ourselves and everyone else. It is what we would like to think of ourselves as being. Everyone has a mask affecting his perceptions of himself. Indeed, we have usually lived with our masks so long that we fail to recognize them for what they are. I recommend it as a useful exercise to try to draw the lineaments of your own mask.

Actually others are less taken in by our masks than we are. A mask, in the psychological as in the material sense, is rigid, unchanging, and contrived. What we *do*, however, belies what we are trying to *be*, and often contradicts the pretensions of the mask. When this is the case and people fail to take us at our mask value, we feel severely menaced. If the mask fails to protect us we are threatened anew by whatever it was constructed to save us from.

One remedy for this situation is the mirage. If this word arouses an image of water and waving palm trees, it can be forgotten: mirages in the desert are livid, shimmering, and palpably deceitful. I use the word in its true sense of a false image, and that is precisely what we see, squinting through the slits of the mask. We see our enemies, associates, and friends in the very shapes and shades we had obscurely sensed to be our own but had, through the use of the mask, repudiated and denied. The mask, in short, enables us to see in others what we fear to see in ourselves (the mirages) and to see an equally unreal but this time idealized picture of our own person.

As with awareness in general, mask and mirage formation fluctuates continually, being weak when stress is low or awareness is high, and strong when the opposite conditions prevail.

It has a social as well as a personal dimension. I have encountered this on the occasions when I have been involved in negotiations relating to international conflict. In those circumstances it is usually referred to as the mirror-image effect. Each side makes the same accusations about the other and claims the same virtues for itself: '*We* are peace-loving, *they* are aggressive; *our* soldiers abide by the rules of war, *theirs* are little better than hired assassins; *we* have offered generous terms, *they* refuse to negotiate; *we* only want justice, *they* want to destroy us.' Although the officials who make such statements may have less distorted perceptions in their personal relationships, it may be that the same core of anxiety that is activated by the stress of war also gives rise to more individual mask–mirage formation.

3 Identity

Anyone who employs the concept of identity stands upon the shoulders of Erik Erikson, a position both privileged and presumptuous. I acknowledge my stance with humility. Yet, as Erikson says, the problem of identity is 'all pervasive', being concerned with a 'process located *in the core of the individual* and yet *also in the core of his communal culture*' (Erikson, 1968, p. 22). I dare to believe that there is room for additional approaches to this omnipresent issue and hope that what I have to say, while not inconsistent with Erikson's views, may contribute something to the discussion.

We have already seen that the mask–mirage function contributes, by *reaction*, to a man's self-image: if they (the others) are bad then we, by contrast, are good, and the worse they are, the better we are. In this chapter I discuss two other modes of self-definition. Both can properly be termed facets of identity, but to differentiate them I refer to one as belonging-identity and to the other as awareness-identity. Briefly, belonging-identity implies that we define ourselves in terms of what we belong to or what belongs to us. We are the sum total of our affiliations. Awareness-identity implies that we define ourselves in terms of what our level of awareness reveals about our nature.

Just as the level of awareness fluctuates, so, and very largely in accordance with it, does the balance of the two forms of identity. When belonging-identity is in the ascendant, awareness-identity is low and, of course, the other way about. The various combinations of the two types of identity with various levels and types of awareness determine in large measure the response to the social situation: withdrawal, apathy, militancy, mysticism, conservatism, reaction, or progressiveness.

BELONGING-IDENTITY

I shall begin with an issue which, if not made clear, could do considerable damage to my argument. It has been suggested to me that belonging-identity should be valued as a necessary precondition of concern for, or commitment to, people or causes. If this were so, a weakening of this form of identity would imply a weakening of responsibility towards them. But I believe that the reverse is true. Within the context of belonging-identity, as I define it, people are primarily important to us because they help us to build it up. We appreciate them not so much for themselves as for enabling us to see ourselves in a better light: to the extent to which they 'belong' to us or we to them, we are helped to build the shell of identity without which we should be so vulnerable. Conversely, the less we depend upon them in this manner, the more we are able to appreciate and to understand – to be aware of – them and their needs.

If we ask ourselves the existential question, 'Who am I?' – and that we do it so infrequently indicates how low the average level of awareness is – we have to admit that we respond largely in terms of belonging. We must recognize, even if it shames us to do so, that we owe our sense of three-dimensionality, our feelings of worth, certainty, solidity, reality, and comfort in times of stress, to things outside ourselves or at least not of our making. First of all, perhaps, there is a deep sense of belonging to culture, or civilization. Thus speaks Freud, as quoted by Erikson:

> 'What bound me to Jewry was (I am ashamed to admit) neither faith nor national pride, for I have always been an unbeliever and was brought up without any religion, though not without respect for what are called the 'ethical standards' of human civilization. Whenever I felt an inclination to national enthusiasm, I strove to suppress it as being harmful and wrong, alarmed by the warning examples of the peoples among whom we choose to live. But plenty of other things remained over to make the attraction of Jewry and Jews irresistible – many

obscure emotional forces, which are the more powerful the less they can be expressed in words, as well as clear consciousness of inner identity, the safe privacy of a common mental construction. And beyond this there was the perception that it was to my Jewish nature alone that I owed two characteristics that have become indispensable to me in the difficult course of my life. Because I was a Jew I found myself free from many prejudices which restricted others in the use of their intellect; and as a Jew I was prepared to join the Opposition, and to do without agreement with the "compact majority" ' (Erikson, 1968, pp. 20–1).

I should make it clear that I am not suggesting that everyone who shares the same spectrum of belonging (to the extent that this is possible) will have a similar identity. There are other factors, such as infantile experience, which shape us, which give our personality a particular configuration and particular strengths and weaknesses. These determine the way in which we select the items of belonging that are most significant to us, pattern them, and arrange them in hierarchies of importance. But although we all organize our world of belonging differently, we all rely on it equally for support and confirmation.

My personal inclination is to deny that I am dependent on a belonging-identity. I should like to think that I rely entirely (as, like the rest of us, I probably do in part) on awareness-identity. But honest introspection shows that this is not so. When assailed by doubt and uncertainty, I find nuggets of comfort in a few of my personal and professional achievements. Surely I can't be so bad (or stupid, or useless) if . . . ? What I have done, the positions I have held, the books I have written, the missions I have undertaken, the people who have admitted me to their confidence or intimacy, become more me than what I actually am. (In one sense, one cannot separate these two. What I am determines what I do; what I do contributes to what I am. But in the last analysis, externals and self are different.) I recall that at one stage, if things were not going well with my work, I had a core of reassurance that would make me feel happier, removing the threat to my identity. For some time I did not trouble to analyse this core. Then I realized that it was my membership of a particular learned society, which meant, I hoped, that I could not be as stupid as I sometimes feared I was. Although I was perfectly aware that I had been most gratified by my election to it, I had concealed from myself the fact that it meant so much.

It is undoubtedly easier to build up and maintain a strong sense of belonging-identity in a stable society. In days when patriotism was natural and universal; when class distinctions were clearly defined and when, indeed, one was content with the situation into which God had been pleased to put one; when position, high or low, was hedged around with traditional observances and by the same token hallowed; when the old values retained their force – it was easier to be sure of who one was. One might be the duke or one might be his butler: each took equal pride in his belonging. (Pride, in fact, is essential to belonging-identity.)

First, belonging-identity has a strong conservative streak. It draws strength from and in turn supports the *status quo*. But we live in a society in which values are changing with enormous rapidity, traditions are archaic survivals, and the old social distinctions are largely eroded. This is good in that many of the former oppressions, inequities, and injustices are menaced, but serious problems are created for our own identities. All would be well if we were able to rely on awareness-identity, on the sense of who we are rather than on what we are in terms of our associations (John Smith, a human being with capacities for both shame and glory, rather than a white Anglo-Saxon Protestant stockbroker educated at Eton and Harvard Business School). But this is not easy. Some of us root ourselves absurdly in the past, becoming laughing-stocks through our addiction to the status symbols of a bygone age. Most of us, however, lack the traditional objects of identity, objects that have through time become well organized into coherent structures, such as the privileges and the duties of a butler. In consequence, we search rather desperately for new sorts of belongingness.

I was impressed recently in England by the extent to which being the fan of a particular football team had become a part of many people's identity. They formed clubs on that basis, wore rosettes, and put stickers on their cars and even signs in their windows. When they went by train to matches they would sometimes, in a kind of mad excess of solidarity, of belonging to each other, commit fearful acts of vandalism. Throughout the Western world, people for whom there is little meaning in what were, for an earlier generation, the comforts of conventional belonging, are seeking something new and valid to adhere to. The old and the middle-aged still manage, on the whole, to cling to old associations, to feel that there is some shielding virtue in being an alumnus of a particular college, a member of a particular organization or a particular family, to believe that one has a position to be kept up and so on. The young snatch at evanescent cults. Moreover, these cults may even be revolutionary in character, a fact that may seem strange in view of the powerful conservative element in this form of identity. However, if one is prevented by temperament and history from deriving satisfaction from a conventional affiliation, there may be no other choice than an unconventional one, even one that aims to destroy conventional society.

Another powerful element in the construction of identity is materialism. The reason is as follows. If we identify ourselves in terms of what we belong to we are also doing so in terms of what belongs to us. If I take pride in belonging to a well-known family or an exclusive club, I use the possessive pronoun in referring to these as 'my family' and 'my club'. The strength of our belonging-identity derives from the fact that the things that we belong to are our things. They also belong to us. Hence, in the crudest form, our possessions – particularly our land, if some interpretations of the territorial instinct are correct – are important and help to confirm us in our identity. Just as I am reassured by my academic honours, so are others by their estates, bank balances, and portfolios. This is why people suffer so desperately in times of slump and depression: they are losing not only money, which is bad enough, but the confidence and strong sense of identity they derived from their wealth.

I would not wish to give the impression, however, that belonging-identity is necessarily crass. Although the butler may be very materialistic in the ordinary sense of the word, the duke may be highly cultured. Indeed, an important part of his identity may be as a patron of the arts. Belongingness can relate just as well to a select literary circle or a church as to a golf club or the stock exchange. What matters is that one's identity is secured *more in terms of what one belongs to than in terms of what one is*; or, to put it differently, in some measure *one becomes what one belongs to*.

It is perhaps not surprising that when severe and large-scale threats are posed to their belonging-identity, people tend to react with violence. Some of the pogroms and persecutions of the past served not only to obliterate such a threat, but through communal action to reaffirm the solidarity of mutual belonging. Such was the Nazi persecution of the Jews.

In conclusion, belonging-identity tends to be a stabilizing force, though not necessarily so. It may, however, preserve what is bad along with what is good, and what is unjust and discriminating rather than what is wise and temperate. It is also a dangerous and explosive force, erupting into violence if threatened. When peaceful and law-abiding citizens become vindictive and cruel overnight (as when immigrants of another race move into their community), it is because their identity of belonging to a particular community, with all that it represents, is threatened. Paradoxically, what had previously made them well-behaved was this same quality: it was *their* community and they took pride in being good members of it. Belonging-identity is the motive force for xenophobia, for the mindless patriotism of 'my country, right or wrong', for the pseudo-mystical yearning after blood and soil, for the arrogant superiority of the local man over the stranger. It is an attribute, finally, that we all share, and in so doing contribute to the most dangerous dilemmas of the human race.

AWARENESS-IDENTITY

We also possess a measure of awareness-identity which counteracts, to some extent, our belonging-identity. It derives from general awareness and contributes to the more or less organized self-image by which we define ourselves. It can be recognized by its relative unpretentiousness. Whereas belonging-identity is somewhat grandiose, albeit with moods of depressed uncertainty and self-doubt, awareness-identity begins to recognize the contradictions and limitations of our nature. Indeed, the first stages of awareness are precisely those that reveal the most insubstantial identity. But whereas moments of doubt as regards our belonging-identity are shattering and can lead to desperate reactions, awareness-identity is comforting. There is a certain dignity in our recognition of our nature. We no longer have to struggle to convince others, and particularly ourselves, what fine fellows we are. Seeing our own selves and not a deluding protective screen we have placed around them, we can begin to work on them.

One important difference between the two poles of identity is that, in the case of belonging, *our most important possession* (that is, belonging) *is our own identity*. We have to be able to present it as we would like to think it is. But if anything goes wrong, if we receive some shock in our self-evaluation, we suffer greatly. We agonize over the flaws in our nature which have led to this situation and we become hostile to people who have been responsible for our defaced self-image.

It should be borne in mind that people often see us differently from how we see ourselves. The mask we present, or think we are presenting, may not be what pleases others, who may in any case evaluate us by traits of which we are virtually unconscious. In our belonging-identity, in fact, we fluctuate by way of depression and anger between self-satisfaction and guilty self-abuse. Awareness-identity, however, accepts the self, acknowledging the deficiencies without self-recrimination and the strengths without self-adulation.

Awareness-identity is a quality everyone possesses to some extent, just as everyone has a measure of natural awareness. But it can certainly be achieved as a result of purposeful efforts. In order to illustrate the nature of awareness-identity, I may perhaps be allowed to describe some of my own efforts in this direction.

I have begun by attempting to empty my mind of the kaleidoscopic flood of thoughts, images, and feelings. After a while, I have tried to observe myself, my state of mind, my physical sensations, my relationships with the people around me and my feelings about these. I am aware of contradictions, confusions, ridiculous fears, hurt *amour propre*, conceit, and the like. All these pertain to my belonging-identity. If I can observe them, as it were, from outside, they begin to fade. These are the things of which I was made. Now they are gone – who am I? I have a strangely empty feeling. At the same time, I experience relief. There are no more pretences to keep up, no more pointless anxieties to harass me. Having jettisoned these impulses, the minor selves that made up myself, I feel more free. It seems that I can now see more clearly, experience emotion more sharply, think more efficiently. I am not worried that my mask and my belonging-identity have evaporated. I can do without them. I no longer know in the old sense who I am. In the new sense, I am aware of a complexity and diversity that I did not know about, or, if I guessed their existence, that I feared. I know, for example, that there is a strong recurrent tendency to belonging-identity and that I have escaped it only temporarily. But for the time being, while the awareness lasts, I do define myself not in terms of belonging, but in terms of being. I am a man. To the extent that I am aware I am in control of my fate. If I were able to prolong this exercise I might have yet another perception of myself, sensing an identity still harder to put into words.

One good reason why I have chosen to use the word 'aware' rather than 'conscious' or 'self-conscious', or any other possible equivalents, is because of its derivation from a Germanic word meaning 'watchful'. My experiments in developing awareness-identity have been short-lived (though I hope their effects have lasted longer) because after a short while *I have forgotten to observe*, and my belonging-identity has flooded back. It is an exceptionally powerful, natural force to which we are all subject. One way to develop a different type of identity may be by watching its play upon us and substituting a different form of awareness based on the very act of watching. This, I take it, has been the basis of much religious and ethical teaching emphasizing and advocating self-knowledge.

4 Configurations of Awareness and Identity I

I first began to think about awareness and identity when I was trying to understand how people behaved under pressure. I was particularly interested in the ways in which the leaders of conflicting groups viewed each other's motives and interpreted each other's actions. It appeared to me that in such circumstances most people, with a few interesting exceptions, developed a very strong identity derived from belonging to their particular side. They became, for example, passionate Biafrans or Nigerians, whereas previously they had been only lukewarm patriots. The other side became almost exclusively cruel, bestial, treacherous, and malign. Their side (and, by association, they as individuals) became peace-loving, chivalrous, considerate, and generally virtuous. This, as we have seen, I termed the mask–mirage function and noted that it was closely associated with a lowering of awareness as well as an enhanced belonging-identity. The analysis of other unpeaceful relationships (reported in *Making Peace*) suggested that different types or levels of awareness and identity, with the concomitant strong or weak mask–mirage function, were involved in other situations. It also suggested that some of the most serious clashes occurred between individuals or groups with differing configurations of awareness and identity. For example, individuals with a strong belonging-identity perceived and valued things very differently from those with strong awareness-identity. From such observed differences I have abstracted four main psychological types:

1 Low awareness (all modes) : weak belonging-identity and weak awareness-identity : strong mask–mirage.

CONFIGURATIONS OF AWARENESS AND IDENTITY I

2   Low awareness (all modes) : strong belonging-identity, weak awareness-identity : strong mask–mirage.
3a Higher natural or self-conscious awareness : weak belonging-identity, increasing awareness-identity : weaker mask–mirage.
3b Higher supraliminal awareness : weak belonging-identity, increasing awareness-identity : weaker mask–mirage.
4   High awareness (any or all modes) : weak belonging-identity, strong awareness-identity : no mask–mirage.

But before attempting to describe these types and to relate them to action in the field of politics and society, I should like to make the following reservations. Typologies are attractive to their inventor, who is gratified to find that his material can be organized into categories (even if he has invented the categories to fit his material). But he has to remember that people were not created to suit his labels. These are no more than a convenience for the student who is trying to systematize a welter of complex and largely contradictory material; a half-way house to more delicate and subtle understanding. Next, it is important to realize that *people do not belong to types: types are in people.* With regard to the above categories, most human beings oscillate from 1 to 4 and back again several times a day, as a moment's watchfulness of ourselves will confirm. We do, however, have a centre of gravity, a point on the scale to which we most frequently return and where we remain the longest. I suspect that for a large random sample this point would be around 2 or between 2 and 3 (for, of course, there is a continuum rather than a set of separate categories).

This point of balance is often objectified by our value system, which is mainly responsible for our social action. The stronger our belonging-identity and the lower our awareness, the more we tend to support the exploitative network and the more strongly we are motivated by competitive materialism. But this is a generalization and there are exceptions, as we shall note. Likewise, and with the qualifications I have just referred to, the higher the level of awareness coupled with an identity based more on awareness than on belonging, the greater the opposition to the exploitative network and its psychological corollary. The type of opposition, however, depends upon the type of awareness. If awareness is natural or self-conscious, the opposition is more likely to take a militant form – that is to say, to be concrete and practical. If awareness is supraliminal, the opposition is likely to be mystical – that is to say, it will involve self-development rather than social reform.

The following sections examine the nature and functioning of these types.

Configuration 1

The psychological development of some individuals has been so impaired that they have virtually no sense of identity. Obviously they are equally deficient in awareness. The unstable psychopath is an example. He is unpredictable because he has no sense of belonging to give some pattern, however circumscribed, to his existence. People in this category are on the fringe of society, and frequently criminal. They contribute little to the community, either to change or to preserve it. Occasionally they commit senseless acts of destruction. Their most positive social action may be to join bands which delight in such activities as Jew-baiting or, in contemporary England, Paki-bashing. Membership of these packs creates only the most fragile and evanescent identity, and the individuals concerned continue to lead lives of unpatterned violence.

A less vicious manifestation of this failure of development is seen in the sad and unstable misfits, potential suicides, alienated loners, who live unhappy, unproductive lives on the edge of the community. Some may be charming and gentle, like Xavier, or socially militant, like Gwenneth, who are described in the case studies below. Some are what might be termed false hippies in that they adopt the gear and the idiom, but not the philosophy, of the counter-culture. What they have in common is their isolation, their seeming incapacity for deep and lasting involvement with others.

It is interesting to speculate on the frequency of this configuration of low awareness and weak identity. Is it increasing? Unfortunately, statistics on such matters are unreliable. Nevertheless, crimes of violence appear to be growing in number in the more highly 'developed' countries and although these are not all committed by persons in this category (some are rational by-products of lucrative criminal activity), the work of the Gluecks[9] and others suggests that psychological preconditions equivalent to my lack of a sense of identity are involved. Figures relating to psychiatric disturbance are even harder to interpret: we are far more conscious of mental illness than in earlier times and, if for no other cause, admissions to treatment have increased. It is not unreasonable to suppose, however, that contemporary conditions would increase the tendency towards this type.

The incredibly swift changes wrought by advancing technology have destroyed many of the bases of belief, behaviour, and belonging which served as foci for our fathers. In order to retain some stability of identity we all engage in a continual struggle of adaptation and adjustment. It is difficult for most people. It may be almost impossible for those whose background is particularly chaotic and deprived and whose personalities are what is called inadequate – a word that implies a lack of integrative force, of any fixed sense of a worth-while self. The situation is exacerbated in some cases by the ethos of competitive materialism. To the extent that identity is reinforced through success in the scrabble for gain and to the extent that the measure of material success is a criterion of being, those who fall behind are doubly threatened. If they fail, who are they? Some seek confirmation by acts which, however crudely, demonstrate that they exist. A rape or a murder cries from the housetops 'I am'.

CASE STUDIES

James

James is a young man of twenty-six, personable and not unintelligent. He is serving a long prison sentence (his fourth) for a violent attack on an old woman. She had surprised him burgling her house and he attacked her with extraordinary violence. He kicked and punched her, breaking several ribs, then bound and gagged her and proceeded to burn her with a lighted cigarette. When she became unconscious (perhaps he thought she was dead), he went around her home systematically destroying everything that looked attractive or precious. Paradoxically, though there were a number of valuable things in the house, including jewellery, he took only a few dollars from her purse. He was arrested a day or two later while having an expensive meal in a restaurant.

James's father had disappeared when he was very young and he and his mother moved around with apparent aimlessness. Most of her earnings came from acting as a waitress at holiday resorts, but she offered other services to holiday-makers which brought in a little extra as well as James's younger brother. James's education was spasmodic, but he was not a bad student. In later years he used to pose as something of an intellectual and had in fact read somewhat unexpectedly. He was, for example, familiar with the works of Camus and Colin Wilson. He also developed rather ritzy tastes and his attempts to obtain the means of indulging them led him to prison more than once. He hardly ever worked and he had no friends, only a few drinking associates. Together they would cook up schemes, seldom entirely honest and usually impracticable, for making their fortunes. They never worked very well, but James was able to get by from day to day. His dreams of affluence, however, far outran his achievements.

He could be charming, but, as one of his acquaintances said, he never seemed quite genuine: you didn't really know who he was. He was also easily depressed and when in one of his moods would speak with maudlin self-pity about his bad luck. But it was difficult to say the right things to him. He took offence very easily and would fly into deadly rages.

Besides dubious projects for money-making, the only activity that aroused his enthusiasm was that of some extreme political groups, such as the John Birch Society. From his literary gleanings he would propound philosophical justifications for their attitudes and extol their hatred of Negroes, Jews, liberals, communists, and the like. He admired what he called the 'existential realism' of the Nazis.

He had been married, but the marriage lasted only eighteen months. He had had any number of casual relationships but none of them had really amounted to anything much.

He was essentially a loner. He admitted to the psychiatrist who examined him while he was awaiting trial that he felt completely outside society, that he had no interest in anyone or anything. He belonged to no clubs or associations, he despised team games. He felt he was nothing, that he didn't belong.

Xavier

At the age of twenty Xavier dropped out of life. His parents were rather stiff, orthodox, middle-class people, the father a successful pharmacist, and he was the fifth of eight children. He did fairly well in school, and went on to college, but in his third year he quietly left in the middle of the term and disappeared. When his friends were questioned, they said that really nobody knew him well; he certainly hadn't confided in anyone. He was a great joiner of student societies, starting off each time as though this were *the thing* that mattered most in the world. But he was also a great leaver, for his enthusiasm rapidly waned and he would suddenly depart without a word of explanation. This sometimes occasioned much inconvenience as, for example, when he abandoned the college dramatics club the night before a performance in which he was taking a fairly important part. But he never seemed to realize what he had done. He went his own abstracted, rather worried way, intimate with none, until drawn by some new craze.

When he left college his father put private detectives on his track and after several months they caught up with him. It seemed that he had wandered with apparent pointlessness from place to place: here he joined a hippie group, there he did manual work at a monastery, there again he washed dishes at a holiday camp. People liked him: he was gentle and pleasant, if remote, in his manner. But nobody got to know him well because he kept moving on. Always, one day, he just wasn't there. Without a word of explanation or apology he had disappeared and the detectives had a hard time tracing him. When they at length caught up with him they telephoned his father who came as quickly as he could and begged Xavier to come home, or at least to keep in touch.

Xavier listened quietly and then said: 'I'm sorry if you and Mom have been worried. But I don't belong. It's no use. I just don't belong.'

When his father asked him to explain himself he shook his head, looked worried, and said he had to go to the toilet. He left the room and didn't come back. He had disappeared again.

Gwenneth

Gwenneth is a student activist who is superficially similar to Carmen (see p. 60 below). Their intellectual interests and political concerns are much the same, and if you asked them both what they thought about the Vietnam war, the exploitation of the Third World, or South Africa, they would both say pretty well the same things. But there is no fire or attractiveness about Gwenneth, only the force of desperation.

Her tongue is bitter and she taunts and nags those who, in her opinion, are not doing what they should. She is an angry person who has no friends, male or female, but through sheer persistence she has achieved high office in a very radical student organization. Her associates are rather afraid of her because she is completely ruthless about people, having no feeling for them as human beings, and regarding them solely as political animals who serve or oppose the causes she believes in.

Yet her tough exterior conceals a frightened and almost cringing person. She once broke down in her tutor's office, sobbing out a miserable story of loneliness and of failure in her human relationships. She said that her work with the organization was the only thing that had given her any sense of identity or self-realization, a feeling of being someone. She seemed glad to have a listening ear, but the next time she came to see her tutor it was to revile him angrily for being a lackey of the establishment.

I have included this sketch of Gwenneth because she illustrates the principle that by no means all militants are people of higher awareness. She is certainly muddled and confused about herself and, radical though she is, hers is a belonging-identity – and even so it is fragile. There is a constant core of anger within her and by joining the organization she has effected a coincidence between her personal rage at life and objective reasons for dissatisfaction. This has provided her with something to establish her identity. To this extent she has been slightly more successful than James or Xavier, but she is a troubled person, a danger to herself and to others.

Configuration 2

This is a vast and diverse category. It embraces rich and poor, Harvard professors and illiterate peasants, the aristocracy and their serfs, Muslims and Hindus, legislators and the dupes who elected them. To describe it is, in a sense, like describing the whole of humanity since it perhaps exemplifies the median mode of feeling.

The essence of the low awareness/strong belonging-identity configuration is that, since awareness is in general too low for awareness-identity to exist, we must rely for our sense of being on our belonging-identity. We become what we belong to and what belongs to us: our civilization, our nation, region, family, church, political party, wife and children, school, university, neighbourhood community, house, land, books, profession, clubs and societies, social standing, investments, tastes in music and literature, views on the meaning of life and the immortality of the soul, preference for brands of cigarettes or gin, friends, reputation, style of dress, eccentricities, honours, hobbies, way with the opposite sex, pictures, and a thousand other things. From these we fabricate a sense of self, an identity. It is by this that we define ourselves to ourselves. It is from these components that we pattern an image of which, when our attention turns towards ourselves, we are conscious.

It is this form of awareness that we must be emptied of in order to achieve the objective self-awareness of the observer.

Awareness, indeed, is something of a threat to those who have developed a strong belonging-identity. It involves breaking images and reconstructing them, a painful, difficult, and often anxious process in which the reassurance of identity is abandoned. One does not, therefore, discuss or question the assumptions on which identity is built up. One cherishes them. They become wrapped around with a certain sanctity. When one aspect of an individual's identity, such as patriotism and a sense of nationality, is shared with many others, it develops a rich and complex mystique. Take, for example, the identity of a typical English gentleman of a few decades ago. This included prominently membership of the established Church of England and citizenship of the British Empire. Such a man would take pride in being 'a good churchman', would regularly attend divine service, act as a churchwarden, and even on occasion invite the vicar (usually his social inferior) to lunch. But he would never discuss spiritual issues. I remember in my own youth being reproved for starting a religious discussion at dinner: 'I'm sorry, but we never talk about religion here.' Nevertheless, many of the people who were not prepared to countenance a religious discussion were interested in politics or art, literature or music, and perfectly ready to talk about them: they were not so central to the identity of 'gentleman'. The same with the Empire. This concept stirred deep emotion and everyone felt increased by association with those who ruled the 'lesser breeds without the law'. Theirs was a 'sacred mission' and anyone who questioned the absolute rightness of imperialism might well have expected to be horse-whipped on the steps of his club. (This is an awkward circumstance: if you took it passively or ran away you were branded as a coward; if you resisted you were a cad who couldn't take his medicine.) It is this absolute certainty of correctness, deriving from the imperative of believing in one's affiliations, that defines establishment. When we spell the word with a capital E we refer to rulers, resenting them because of their power over us. But every community, trade, or group has its establishment of people who stand out because they hold the mystique in its purest form and have, in fact, taken to its logical extreme this particular communal aspect of the belonging-identity. Charismatic leaders tend to be those in their particular establishment (which may even be a revolutionary party!) who are able in their persons to crystallize the focus of belonging. Thus Winston Churchill perfectly represented Englishness, as it was conceived in the 1940s. De Gaulle equally represented *la France*. Their own certainty of the rightness of the things they belonged to constituted a great reassurance to their followers, who for this reason accorded them all the greater support. Charisma, in fact, is a combination of power and passion in self-preservation.

This configuration of awareness and identity is, it need hardly be said, in general conservative. If one's sense of who one is depends on what one has, it is naturally important to preserve it. Since what one has is not merely a matter of personal possessions but of culture, traditions, and values, there is a tendency for people who are predominantly of this configuration to be politically on the right. This is not simply a matter of wealth or social position. The butler will be as staunch a conservative as the duke, indeed he could hardly be a butler if he were not of this persuasion. Moreover, his position in the establishment of the ducal household offers him, unless he should raise his social sights, a very satisfying identity. But even the slave may be a conservative. Like the unfortunate fellow in the parable who buried his one talent rather than lose it, he is conservative because he has so little. But there is one fundamental similarity between him and the duke, who is conservative because he has so much: they both lack awareness and they seek a sense of identity by identification with what they belong to. The slave, should he become aware that he is a slave, as Lenin said, would already be half-free; he is a slave now because he is unaware of what he really is and of the fact that he could be something different.

Somewhere between the slave and the duke are, in all probability, most readers of these pages. To the extent that we are conservative the reason is neither that we have a great deal to lose nor that we have so little that we cling to it in fear. It is simply that our psychological and material self-interest depends upon maintaining things as they are. It is very important to emphasize, however, that this conservative bias is not necessarily reflected in political action or affiliation. It is more a technique of locating and defining ourselves in the world than an ideology. This technique may be applied by those who are left-wing politically as well as by those who are right-wing. The worker who yearns to overthrow the elite and share in their riches may be (though by no means necessarily is) constructing an identity on what he feels *should* belong to him rather than on what *does* already. There is little psychological difference between him and his reactionary neighbour.

Another radical type in this generally conservative configuration is the revolutionary whose sense of belonging actually derives from his membership of the revolutionary group. He may have been someone who found difficulties in establishing a belonging-identity and needed the clear objective, the comradeship, and the relatively simple structure of the group. He may, more complicatedly, have retracted from the uncertainties and ambivalences of revolutionary work undertaken out of higher awareness and some degree of awareness-identity. What is confusing in this case is that he continues to do the same things that he did before, but whereas formerly he acted out of awareness of both himself and the social system, now he responds to an inner need for stable belonging – and what he belongs to is the revolutionary movement. His inner change will, however, almost certainly affect his behaviour. He will be more rigid, more doctrinaire. The structure and survival of the group will be more important to him than its achievements. Whereas he began to work out of altruism, he will now be more interested in himself than in others.

People in this configuration who have a secure belonging-identity are what might be called well adjusted. Indeed, when adjustment was considered as a goal of psychiatric treatment the objective was, essentially, to build a firm belonging-identity which would enable people to function happily and effectively in their circumstances, *whatever they were*. People of this sort are in general well satisfied with their lives. Their principal craving is for more belonging to confirm and further strengthen their identities. If their creed is in general liberal and humanitarian, they will be tolerant, except of what might impair their belonging. If their belonging is menaced, however, they will react strongly, frequently in a fashion that completely belies their professed beliefs and ideals. There will be a violent and acquisitive effort to strengthen belonging and this may well involve ruthless suppression of scapegoats who can be blamed for the tarnished image, or of anyone who appears to be a threat. Unfortunate minority groups, racial or religious, are particularly likely to get caught in this vicious backlash of threatened identity. It is a sad commentary on much of humanity that we find it easier to protect our sense of identity by attacking others than by developing an awareness which would both forge closer ties with them and establish us more firmly within ourselves.

In mitigation it should be said, however, that a great deal of solidarity derives directly from this configuration of awareness and identity. This is quite apart from the satisfaction of being accepted, of belonging to a group, of being one of the boys, one of the gang. We have all experienced it: the sense of comradeship or neighbourliness, the feeling of identity with those who belong to the same organization, college, community, town, and so on, for no other reason than that they belong to it, the acceptance of obligation to them and the services undertaken without question on their behalf – these are positive by-products of belonging-identity. Every time (for whatever inner motive) we help our neighbours, that is the members of *the group to which we belong*, we strengthen our belonging-identity. We are able both to view ourselves more favourably in this identity, thereby enhancing it, and to strengthen the ties of belonging, thereby protecting it. But the other side of this coin is that belonging, to be effective, must be finite. At some point we come to the boundary beyond which the people do not belong to us or we to them. We stop short of accepting into our sphere of identity homosexuals, Negroes, Jews, members of another political party or religion, people from the next town, county, or state: we are not aware of them as human beings. These are the people on whom we turn with violence when our identity is in jeopardy. It is in this sense that low awareness coupled with belonging-identity is a powerful element in most wars and in the situations of mass prejudice and violence that readily lead to them.

People have pointed out to me that my definition of belonging-identity seems to include all human associations and thus that I seem to be suggesting that they are in some way unnecessary or undesirable. But, it is objected, are we not essential to each other? What of loving relationships, the sense of family, deep commitment to the values of one's community? My response is that these things exist more outside the context of the belonging-identity. That form of identity has to be considered as a sort of citadel, constructed out of various elements of affiliation, to which we retreat when threatened by the guilts and anxieties arising from low awareness. We may include in this identity the people who 'belong' to us – husbands, wives, children, neighbours – but our need for them in this capacity is not because they fulfil or complement our natures, give us joy through their sheer existence, stimulate our creativity, or awaken undemanding affection and respect; it is because our fears and uncertainties are assuaged by what they do for us. Our children are intelligent and our wives attractive and this makes us feel better, our self-doubt is fleetingly diminished; we are good to them and that too makes us feel better. What is worse, we manipulate them, we manœuvre them into a position of submission which heightens our diminished sense of power, or in some other way bolsters our fragile ego. In this we are thinking of ourselves, not of them. We may love them too, but this aspect of the relationship is not loving because a large part of loving involves wanting something for the other person, not for ourselves. If we love people we also need them, but so that we may complete ourselves through loving them.

Similar sorts of arguments may be made about community affiliation. One may use one's belonging as part of the shielding identity that protects one from low awareness, which is essentially *selfish*, even though it may lead to community service because one's identity includes the image of the good neighbour and one likes to see oneself in this role. It is a very different thing to be objectively proud of one's community, to admire what it stands for, to respect its values, to revere its traditions, and to love its members. In this sense one's community is very important and it contributes to the common purpose of man, which is to seek for union.

It has also been pointed out to me that it is essential to the emotional growth of children that they should feel part of a group, especially, of course, the family; indeed, that at a very early age they do not articulate the difference between themselves and their mothers. Clearly this is true, though it is perhaps incorrect to equate these infantile feelings with belonging-identity. To the extent that there is some similarity between them, it might be the case – and here I speak with extreme diffidence – that the belonging-identity protracts inappropriately into maturity, creating the ills I have referred to, a stage that was functional in infancy.

I might fleetingly observe that in a more general sense I have played with the idea of relating my configurations of awareness and identity to developmental stages. On the whole I do not see them sequentially and I find no relationship between them and the stages described by Jung, Freud, Piaget, or others. It does appear to me, however, that supraliminal awareness is equivalent to the type of development that Jung believed to be essential to health in the third quartile of man's life. At this stage, Jung said, a man must turn from a life devoted to externals, such as raising a family and establishing himself professionally, and cultivate his inner existence if he is not to fall a victim to depression. But this is no argument against heightened awareness in earlier years.

The mask–mirage function relates closely to the belonging-identity. In my terms it is axiomatic that when awareness is low this mechanism is vigorously employed. Its association with the belonging-identity makes it stronger because it enables us to differentiate with greater clarity between what is part of our belonging complex and what is not. This is largely the function of the mirage. At the same time the mask, the self-image we construct to counteract what we fear within ourselves, is the coagulant for the identity. In one sense, obviously, mask and belonging-identity are one, but the outer mask mechanism provides the inner drive to organize the elements of belonging into presentable form. If mirage formation is what is psychoanalytically termed projection, then mask formation is introjection: we become the things we belong to and define ourselves in terms of them.

It is the combination of low awareness and strong belonging-identity that provides the mainspring for the exploitative network and for competitive materialism. It is not hard to see why. This configuration is very largely materialistic. It depends to a great extent on what is external, visible, measurable, and can be given a value. I say to a great extent rather than completely because the elements of belonging include many things, such as patriotism, culture, and social tradition, which are not materialistic in the conventional sense as are possessions and social status. They are, however, adjuncts of an identity in which they play the same part as the more obviously material elements and can be clearly distinguished from the inward vision which constitutes awareness-identity.

Belonging-identity depends, then, on the preservation and indeed the development of what belongs to us and what we belong to. Much of this must involve, in the most crass sense, material stability or, preferably, gain. This does not mean that we are all money-grubbers; we may be highly cultured and despise the business treadmill. But in wealthy societies we have costly tastes, and the satisfaction of the literary, musical, or artistic sides of our identity is likely to involve things that ultimately demand injections of hard cash: concerts, art galleries, books, records, pictures, antiques, furniture, musical instruments, *objets d'art*, etc. And, of course, much of our identity is directly dependent upon the products of the exploitative network. According to our professed social ideology we may or may not deplore it, but we profit from it to reinforce our identities. Our jobs, our investments, and our purchases all strengthen the hold of the rich over the poor, but they also augment our identities (though at certain stages they may cause conflict) and we are not prepared to sacrifice them.

Competitive materialism is more the ideology of this configuration than of any other. Materialistic, because it is through measurable or observable material achievements that, failing any inner measure, we can identity ourselves and others can identify us. Competitive because, if material success is the yardstick, the identity is reinforced if we have more belongings – a higher standard of living, more university degrees, a better collection of gramophone recordings, more valuable paintings, a larger house, a newer car, children who go to a better school, and so on and so on – than our neighbour. Thus the conjunction of this awareness/identity configuration with competitive materialism is a driving force in raising the material quality of living (for many) and in scientific and technological progress.

But both the exploitative network and competitive materialism are sources of strife, bitterness, suffering, tyranny, victimization, inequality (for the essence of competition is that some succeed at the expense of others), violence, and wars.

For these reasons, the combination of low awareness and strong belonging-identity, which we almost all manifest and to which we almost all contribute, is a lethal element in human society. Its values and assumptions – that belonging matters, that certain sorts of material achievements and possessions are in themselves good, and that their preservation is more important than anything else – are so widespread that the greater part of humanity does not question them. Yet it is these that lead us to destruction. It is about them that the cold war, and most hot ones, are fought. I am not positing an aggressive instinct in man. It is hardly necessary to do so. It is enough to say that people tend to react aggressively when the security of their belonging-identity is threatened. What has been termed the territorial imperative is, I believe, only a clearly defined element in belonging-identity.

ILLUSTRATIONS

It is not possible to provide case studies illustrating this configuration. For one thing, the person of low awareness and strong belonging-identity is Everyman. He is a large part of every militant and mystic (though a smaller part of those who have achieved more awareness-identity). If I were to illustrate him by pen pictures it would suggest that there was a type or types. There are types of mystics, militants, and the rest, and I am not against trying to establish them by presenting portraits of those who best exemplify them. But one cannot type a norm that transcends all bounds of class, culture, religion, race, nationality, sex, and historical period. Almost every story in the press deals with it, almost every TV feature, most books of fiction or history.

I had thought to present several cases. A professor (perhaps myself), delighting in his identity as an academic, reassured by the sight of a row of his publications on the bookshelf, reassured by the approval of his students who like his mildly radical approach (on which he also compliments himself).

Or a tough, uneducated construction worker, built up by the *esprit de corps* of a group who face common danger on the high girders, inflamed by an angry patriotism against commies and unwashed hippies and people who talk about peace, glad to see himself as a fan of the Mets or the Sox, proud of his colour TV set.

Or again, an unhappy Sindhi peasant whose major identity is, virtually, that he is a serf and belongs to his landlord, reinforcing this identity by carrying out the traditional observances at weddings, funerals, and similar occasions – or perhaps breaking out of his miserable rut and joining some messianic sect such as the Hurrs.

Or the duke I have mentioned before who, in the truest sense, *is* his family tradition, his culture, his exquisite taste, his collection of French Impressionists, his humanely liberal principles.

And then his butler, who is just as proud *to be a butler* (not John Smith, a human being), the chief factotum of the household, who sets more store on dignity than does the duke himself, who has, after all, a wider sphere of interests and influence.

Or the good physician whose identity consists mainly of being just that (which is largely what is meant by being wedded to one's job).

And perhaps the small-town citizen, busy and respected and full of good works, member of a dozen committees, confidant of the mayor, a Rotarian, a good neighbour – and happy to see himself as a combination of all these things.

And a musician identified with his art, a teacher with his school, a minister with his church, a politician with his party, a scientist with his research, and so on, literally, *ad infinitum*.

But these models are really not much help. They are still, in a sense, caricatures. We can look at them and feel that we are different, superior, but they are we.

The things they–we belong to (or that belong to them–us) are different. What is the same is the dependence on this belonging and the reaction to threats to the belonging. This reaction actually may range from depressed self-doubt and anxiety to anger, desperation, rejection of the threat, and violence: what all its manifestations have in common is its negative quality.

If we wish to understand this configuration, the best way is to look in the mirror. But, paradoxically and hopefully, the more clearly we recognize it, and ourselves manifesting it, the more rapidly it fades and changes.

5 Configurations of Awareness and Identity II

Configurations 3a and 3b

As I have mentioned already, most of us pass through most stages or configurations of awareness and identity several times a day. Now we are enslaved by a deadly shaft of anxiety and, self-absorbed in our distress, see others through a mist of pain as the cause of our troubles. Now we are detached, observant, ironical, and objective. Now we have an almost blinding flash of insight. Then again our vision muddies. We do not like to believe that we pass through these vicissitudes. We have constructed a mask of constant benevolent wisdom – or something equally complimentary – the components do not matter. What matters dangerously is our belief in the permanency and unchangeability of the mask, because this belief impedes our efforts to achieve greater awareness. But honest introspection will show how false it is. There are, however, a large number of persons whose centre of psychological gravity is in this particular configuration of higher awareness and weak belonging-identity, accompanied by an emerging awareness-identity. Many of these are the middle-class educated young. Middle class because they have not had the sort of struggle to survive that can lead to an overrating of material circumstances. Educated because, whatever the flaws of the various systems, education gives one a chance to stand back observantly from life and to make contact with seminal ideas. Young because they have not yet become dependent on the belonging system of the exploitative network and competitive materialism. I am clearly not excluding other people, of a different age, social background, or educational level, from this category. Certainly, such

CONFIGURATIONS OF AWARENESS AND IDENTITY II

people are represented in it and the proportion may be increasing, but this configuration is to some extent a class and generational one whereas low awareness/strong belonging-identity is universal, including rich and poor, aristocrat and peasant, educated and illiterate, old and (though in somewhat smaller numbers) young.

This is why so many of those young people whose awareness is higher are at odds with their parents and most of their teachers: their awareness/identity configuration is different, they value different things, they have different purposes, and their visions of themselves and of the world are incompatible with those of their parents and teachers.

As the level of awareness rises, the belonging-identity inevitably weakens. Concomitantly, awareness-identity begins to develop, but it too is weak. This is a painful and difficult intermediate stage. We begin to observe, to be aware of ourselves as ourselves, and at the same time our props and supports of belonging begin to crumble. *We no longer know who we are.* All we are certain of is that our earlier self-image was a false one and that our view of the world deriving from that self-image was equally wrong. This is a configuration characterized by loneliness and insecurity, by confusion and strain. Old associations based on mutual belonging rather than on love tend to break down, and we feel lost and uneasy. We are unstable because we have not yet developed the values by which to orient and steer ourselves. At the same time, this is a stage of liberation. The sense of relief from conformity, and from deadening habits of thought and social behaviour is overwhelming. But we are not quite free. We oscillate between dependence and liberty, convention and freedom.

Our sense of identity – both modes – is most imperfect. We are gauche, ill-at-ease with those who feel differently, over-emphatic in our insecurity, moody, silent, falsely diffident, unsure of ourselves, bragging and ranting to compensate, prone to exaggerate, suspicious, prickly, frightened, frantic. This is an unstable configuration because the stresses of our weak awareness-identity may push us back to our belonging-identity or even to the nihilism of low awareness/low belonging-identity. We seek the company of our kind and there it is easier for us to be gay, open, and relaxed, and, in relative safety, to begin to construct a new identity. But the hidden danger here is that dependence on the group restores the importance of belonging.

There is a strong sense of desperation at this stage. We are between the buttressed complacency of identity based on belonging and the assured inner tranquillity of awareness-identity. We are desperate, first, because of our own lack of roots. We are frightened and vulnerable because we are on our own and have no secure sense of belonging. We are desperate, further, because of what our awareness reveals about the world. We are surrounded by enormities about which we can do so little – bristling armouries of poised nuclear weapons, the hidden horrors of chemical and bacteriological warfare, pollution arising from man's rapacity and indifference, a thousand forms of exploitation and political repression, the heavy smog of materialism and the antihuman values it spawns.

The desperation is not constant, however. It alternates with something like peace. At least we know what the issues are. We have begun to be aware of *what we are not*, even though awareness-identity has not developed to the point where we know *what we are*. We know we are beginning – telling phrase – to find ourselves and are no longer quite such accurate reflections of the norms and values of the wider society. We are at the edge of autonomy. This enables us, at times, to act with great courage and power, to defy overwhelming authority, to be wise and compassionate. But we cannot yet be consistent in these things.

It is at this stage that there is a split in the type of awareness. In some, the increased awareness is natural or self-conscious. In others it is supraliminal, *or it purports to be*. Identity in both is rudimentary.

HIGHER NATURAL OR SELF-CONSCIOUS AWARENESS (3a)

When the higher awareness is of this character, social action is likely to be militant and, as it were, secular. There may still, however, be a wide range of manifestations, including the toughly cerebral, as in the case of a Bertrand Russell, the compassionate warmth and care for the unfortunate of an Abbé Pire,[10] and the revolutionary ardour of a Fidel Castro. Most student activists would come into this category (provided, naturally, that their enthusiasm did spring from awareness rather than from the need to belong to an organization).

I am not, of course, suggesting that everyone within this configuration is a social militant in any definable sense. I am, however, talking about those people who, if their convictions developed and their insights became clear enough to impel them to take a stand, would follow what I term the *external road*. They hold that society is to be changed by changing, or in some cases destroying, its institutions, and, if they take any positive action, this is what they will try to do. By contrast, those who are striving for supraliminal awareness will take the *inner road*. Their purpose is to achieve an internal change in themselves which will help them eventually to change society, though in much less clearly specified ways. Jung might have referred to these two approaches as introverted and extroverted.

There is an important distinction to be made concerning those who undertake social action as a result of natural or self-conscious awareness: this is between those who are prepared to work within the system to change it and those who believe that it can be changed only from outside.

Those who are prepared to work within the system tend to be older and more established, and hence they have, or think they have, some leverage in society. They fear the implications of revolution and prefer the route of evolution. The criticism that may be levelled against them is that they are deceiving themselves: for those in power will never permit changes to occur constitutionally which might damage their interests. It might further be added that they are still sufficiently enmeshed with their belonging-identity to wish to cling to things that establish that identity; that their perception of the need for change is intellectual, even conventional, rather than felt. However, it could be argued, on the contrary, that in these people belonging is weak and conviction strong, but their perception of the best – and least painful – way of achieving change is different from that of those who decide to work from outside the system; in other words, the two approaches simply reflect different interpretations of the social and political realities.

Those who believe that institutional change can be achieved only from without are often younger and have lower social position – many, in fact, are students. They do not see how they can influence the course of events from inside. In order to do so they would have to achieve power within the system and this they conceive to be corrupting – once in it, they would no longer wish to change it. These people constitute the hard core of the real revolutionaries. Among student activists they make up the left-wing of the Students for a Democratic Society, and such groups as the Maoists, the Weathermen, and the Progressive Labour Party. They believe in the most extreme attacks on the existing order, indeed on its destruction. Only thus, they would affirm, can the cancer of imperialism and capitalism be burnt out.

Here it is important to distinguish between the revolutionary and his ideology. Some embrace violence with great reluctance, only because they are intellectually convinced that the suffering it entails for the few is justified by the advantage that would accrue to the many from the establishment of a just and egalitarian society. They are activated by a passionate concern for the human misery caused by the exploitative network. Personally they are warm and open, and have great insight into the human condition. Such a one was Che Guevara. They are people whose level of awareness and sense of identity are above average for this category.[11]

There are others, however, who are outwardly similar but inwardly, I believe, very different. They share the same political beliefs, they belong to the same groups and take part in the same revolutionary activities, but their awareness level is much lower: they may even be verging towards low awareness/weak belonging-identity. Consequently their motives are different. They tend to have strong mask–mirage functions and, while they see themselves as revolutionary heroes, delight to brand their enemies as pigs who deserve nothing but slaughter. In the same way, their sense of identity is weak, so weak that there may be little except the revolutionary group for them to realize themselves through. Hence they are as likely to visit their professor's office to weep in desperation as they are to shout obscenities at him and splash his papers with ink. These people should more properly be considered as belonging to Configuration 1.

There is a third group who believe in radical social change, in revolution rather than reform, but by non-violent means. Among these, too, it is possible to find rather desperate individuals of low awareness who find some identity in the movement, but the majority appear to be people of relatively high awareness.

Does non-violence indicate a higher level of awareness, a deeper sympathy, than violence? I would not wish to pass judgement on this matter. I suspect that there are temperamental factors involved as well as ideological ones. I, for example, would find it hard, if not impossible, to choose a violent way of changing society and in consequence I have forged myself an ideology to support my natural inclinations – or is it the other way round? I would suspect, however, that whatever the temperamental differences, there is more in common between a tough apostle of violent revolution, such as Che, and an equally tough proponent of non-violent social change, such as George Lakey,[12] than between either of these and activists of low awareness.[13]

This is not the place to discuss the pros and cons of violent revolution. It is a much-debated philosophical and practical issue which is not germane to the principal arguments of this book. I might mention, however, that there are certain approaches to violence that seem to me incompatible with a high level of awareness. If it is vindictive or vengeful; if it is not carried out to achieve a specific social goal; if it simply aims to reverse the social system by making the top dogs the bottom dogs and the bottom dogs the top dogs; if there is no thought of conversion as a desirable substitute for killing – then the militants' level of awareness is low and their sense of identity is weak. In their revolutionary work they are serving their own psychological ends rather than an altruistic goal of changing society for the eventual good of all.

The militant who owes his activism to his concern for others rather than himself is serious, but capable of gaiety. He holds strong political and social views, but he is not a narrow dogmatist and is prepared to change his position if given good reason to do so. This is the case whether he works within or outside the system, violently or non-violently.

Frank

He is a university research worker who has flung himself with extraordinary zeal into the American civil rights movement. White himself, he is deeply committed to the cause of the blacks, knows most of the leading black spokesmen and, what is most unusual, is trusted by them. His father was a minister in a poor parish in a Chicago slum, a saintly, tough, quiet, dedicated man who cared more for his vocation than his family and passed his convictions on to his children, accustoming them from an early age to understand what poverty and discrimination really mean to those who are subjected to them. There was not much fun in the home. There was no money, for one thing – every spare penny went to some good cause – and for another, every spare quantum of energy or emotion was directed to some form of useful service. One's response to this sort of background is usually extreme. One either rejects it utterly, or accepts it completely. Frank did the latter. His eyes were opened and he could not forget the miseries of the poor.

At college, where he was a brilliant student, he graduated in physiology which he had studied because he wanted to work on problems of deficiency diseases connected with poverty. After getting his Ph.D. he obtained a good research appointment, but he became increasingly involved with political issues and spent more and more of his time organizing demonstrations, advising the black leaders on their approach to the authorities, and trying to involve his colleagues in the civil rights movement.

Eventually he was spending so little time in his laboratory that the head of his department protested. Frank answered with surprised indignation that he had taken up the study of nutrition and deficiency illnesses to help the black population, but that his present semi-political work was equally necessary to bring about an improvement in conditions and should therefore be encouraged. The head of the department, a mild and reasonable man, replied with restraint that this was all very well, but what Frank was being paid for was physiological research; by no stretch of imagination could most of his present activities be so described.

Frank became very confused and upset. For several days he did not come to work at all and confided to a friend that he had neither slept nor eaten during this time. He felt anxious and insecure; nobody understood what he was trying to do. After a week he returned and sought an interview with the head of the department who reported that Frank had seemed very nervous and unsure of himself, had sweated profusely, and had come out with the most extraordinary arguments. There seemed to be a very wide gap between Frank's intellectual brilliance and his penetrating insight into the social situation that so concerned him, and his ability to understand the simplest thing about his position. He was very ill-at-ease in the department, was unable to fit in. Though he inspired admiration, even devotion, and was a passionate and eloquent speaker, he greatly lacked self-confidence. He saw slights where none was intended, read complex insults into the most ordinary remarks, while the slightest criticism sent him almost into a panic which would remove him from the scene, brooding and desperate for days.

All in all, Frank is a clear example of a man whose natural awareness is greater than his awareness-identity, and whose belonging-identity is correspondingly weak. Some things he sees very clearly, but his vision has developed at the expense of his security.

Ted

He is a tough, radical lawyer, most of whose time goes to defending people who, in his opinion, are the victims of discrimination or social injustice of any sort. He is a militant campaigner against the Vietnam war and once actually visited Hanoi with an anti-war group in direct defiance of the State Department. His articles in law journals have marked him as being one of the leading young intellectuals in the profession as well as one of the most revolutionary. Several major universities have offered him chairs, but he prefers to remain free to follow his own interests. He is also somewhat afraid that he would find the atmosphere of the average law school uncongenial and restrictive.

Ted is no gloomy idealist. He is a cheerful extrovert with an enormous number of friends and a great capacity for enjoying himself, but he is quite implacable in his opposition to what he holds to be wrong.

It is interesting to compare Ted with Frank. Ted has a stronger sense of identity, is much less anxious, but less sensitive. He had the advantage of coming from a large, happy, normal middle-class family with intellectual interests and plenty of money. They were always concerned with, but not obsessed by, social questions. Frank, in ordinary clinical terms, is neurotic, while Ted is not. But Frank's neurosis, though no doubt largely the product of his rather grim early environment, seems to be heightened by the way in which he has pushed himself away from all the supports most people enjoy. It is always difficult to cope with raised awareness, but those with stable backgrounds, like Ted, can manage better than those without them.

Carmen

She is a firebrand, a political refugee from one of the Latin American countries where she was a member of a group of revolutionary students. She left after her group had been involved in an armed clash with the police. She was wounded and one of the leaders was killed. On his body papers were found which led the authorities to the headquarters of the group, and after that no one was safe. Carmen was hidden until her wound healed and then smuggled out of the country. Eventually she fetched up in England, where she is enrolled in a university studying, not surprisingly, political science.

Carmen is an attractive girl, fiery and energetic. As soon as her English was good enough she began to take an active part in student politics and quickly became something of a bane to the authorities. She has not the slightest hesitation in marching into the office of the vice-chancellor or the registrar or any appropriate official, eyes flashing, to protest against something or other – usually not unreasonably, and she does it with a certain charm. The other students like and admire her, but are somewhat in awe of her. She stands no nonsense and bullies or shames the laggards into action by the risks she is prepared to take herself.

But for all her flaming militancy there is a diffidence about her, though she seldom shows it openly. Although she has had a succession of man friends she has very few intimates and seems afraid of letting herself go. She became friendly with the family of one of the professors and admitted to his wife that, although she felt passionately about the injustices she protested against, she had to force herself into action. She felt lonely and insecure and tried to seek reassurance, or self-confirmation, from her love affairs, but these did not help very much.

It is not that she is incapable of giving or receiving affection – she and the young revolutionary who was killed had loved each other deeply – but she somehow cannot knit her life as student, revolutionary idealist, and woman into a harmonious whole. She does not know how to define herself.

Charles

Charles is considerably older than the others, about half-way between Professor Noam Chomsky and Dr Benjamin Spock, men who might be considered to represent this configuration at its best. He has a Ph.D. in agricultural economics, and for the past quarter of a century has worked overseas – often in excessively uncomfortable and difficult conditions – on problems of agricultural and indeed general rural development.

As a student collecting material for his thesis in Iran he became sensitized to the miseries of poverty and resolved to devote the rest of his life to alleviating them in so far as he could in his professional capacity. He has kept his resolution. Today, a quiet, grey man who nevertheless has the authority that comes from knowledge and experience, he is a widely accepted expert on land reform and rural society as well as on more technical agricultural questions.

He has been at the job far too long to have any illusions about the altruism of most of the governments or aid agencies with which he has worked. He has seen that land reform, for example, is promoted because it is a fashionable thing and staves off trouble – but it is watered-down land reform of a sort that has virtually no effect on the vested interests of the rich groups who comprise the governments of the countries concerned, and by the same token it has equally little effect upon the conditions of the poor. And he has seen that much foreign aid primarily serves the interests of the donor, and may not be to the long-term advantage of the recipients. Despite this he has remained within the system in the sense that he has worked with official agencies, national and international, rather than independently. He argues that he is thus in a position to have some influence on the course of events and cites examples of situations he has been able to change by persuasion, bullying, or pressure of one sort or another. He also cites jobs he has left in protest.

He maintains that the only alternative for him would be to become a revolutionary, and he admits that he has seen many places that could be changed only through revolution. But he has his own skills, his hardly acquired experience, and a personal diffidence about changing the role which he in fact plays with such ability, toughness, and persistence.

His wife died giving birth, in some god-forsaken spot, to her first child. He has no family, for the child also died soon after. He is worried about what may happen to him when he has to give up his work. 'I don't belong anywhere,' he says.

HIGHER SUPRALIMINAL AWARENESS (3b)

At some stage in the growth of awareness many people become attracted by the idea that it is possible to educate not only the rational intellect, but also the consciousness; that perception of entirely new categories, hard to describe in ordinary language, can be achieved. There are indeed few who have not, at some time, seen the world in an extraordinary new light, seen colours and shapes in such a fashion that they felt themselves to be perceiving the inner meaning of things. Such visions may be fleeting and apparently random (though they may also be associated with illness, hunger, and of course certain drugs), but they make us feel that there is another mode of vision which, perhaps, we could cultivate and control.

Attempts to gain this sort of awareness (which may be successful in some measure – who can say?) are frequently made after there has been a sufficient development of natural awareness to confer sensitivity to the social scene. The increased sensitivity prompts a response. If there is no shift to supraliminal awareness, there is a growing compulsion to do something about society, to be involved. The shift to supraliminal awareness leads, on the other hand, to a compulsion to do something *about oneself*. I would not, of course, suggest that one is either completely militant or completely mystical. In many instances there is a constant oscillation between the poles. Nor is it impossible to effect a certain conscious combination of the two modes: some militants, for example, are austerely self-disciplined in both mind and body. But, as with levels of awareness, there is a centre of gravity. It is seen as more important *either* to change society *or* to change oneself – though the inner change may be seen as an essential preliminary to bringing about social change.

There are, however, many different approaches to supraliminal awareness or, rather, many ways, or ostensible ways, of trying to achieve it. I should make it perfectly clear at once that much that is done in this direction is self-deceptive if not outright bogus. There are fraudulent mystics everywhere, people whose level of awareness is low or whose belonging-identity is defective, who chant mantras, wear bizarre clothes, and make oracular statements because they feel such behaviour is fashionable or they obtain exhibitionistic gratification from it, or because they acquire thereby some evanescent sense of identity. They may not be easy to distinguish from those who look the same, and in many ways behave similarly. But there is a great inner difference between them and the groups we shall shortly be considering. The latter, however strangely – according to middle-class preconceptions – they look and act, are both purposeful and moral. Their morality may be different from ours, but it is frequently more firmly held, since it has developed through a conscious effort to discover right action rather than through unthinking acceptance of an existing social code. Needless to say, it is necessary to know people fairly well before one can distinguish between the true and the false. But, as we shall see, the most serious and genuine efforts can go awry.

I divide the seekers after supraliminal awareness into six groups.

(i) *The Failed Militants*

I describe thus people who have made serious efforts at activism, but have come to believe that nothing remains except a mystical approach. They have come up against the inexorable inertia or hostility of the social system. Or they have found that they lacked the wisdom, courage, or persistence to pursue militant action to the necessary extremes. In either case the interior road has offered an alternative.

The failed militant may follow any route to mystical experience: he may become a drug-taker, a nirvana-seeker, a counter-culture builder, a psycho-philosopher, or a hippie, but this does not mean that every mystic is a former militant. As might be expected, however, those who have first tried a militant approach tend to be the more socially active and organized of the mystics. They found communes, they actively promote the counter-culture, they lecture and teach.

Before going further I should comment that while most of these five modes of seeking supraliminal experience may be combined, some are incompatible. In particular, psycho-philosophy is inconsistent with nirvana-seeking and anything more than minor drug-taking.

(ii) *The Drug-takers*

It is not surprising that supraliminal aspirants have taken so readily to drugs. Ever since Aldous Huxley's *The Doors of Perception* was published (1954), there has been a growing interest in drugs as agents for the expansion of consciousness. This interest was later boosted considerably by the work of Timothy Leary (e.g. Leary, 1968). The mood of youthful dissent began to grow in the early 1960s, so the increasing availability of drugs (albeit for the most part illicit) came at the right moment for those who wanted to find a way out of the ordinary world.

As we have seen, deep despair is felt at the 'inhumanity' and 'soullessness' of modern materialist society. However much we dissent from it, we have inevitably imbibed its modes of perception and lost our capacity to see clearly and feel deeply. But at least we know we have done so and have access to drugs which can restore the impaired vision and the lost bliss. Drugs (some of them some of the time) are prepackaged supraliminal awareness. The following statements demonstrate that drugs (in all these cases, LSD) can have seemingly most desirable effects:

'I was a compulsive thief. I couldn't go into a shop without popping things into my pockets, usually things I didn't want at all. Then I had one dose of LSD. I suddenly saw my life whole and knew I was ruining it. I thought with horror, "What the hell am I doing? I must stop it." And I did. I was really aware for the first time of this craving, or whatever it was, and being aware I no longer wanted to do it – and I haven't. That was three years ago.'

'My sight is bad – so bad that I never really enjoyed looking at things. Then I had this drug and all at once I saw – I really saw. Things are beautiful. The pattern of the grain of wood, the subtle lights in a fold of cloth. I really saw them and though I can't any longer I know they are still there and somehow my perceptual processes have changed.'

'I suddenly saw that everything was one. I was part of the universe and the universe was in me. I was conscious of it in a way which is precise and factual, almost *scientific*, and at the same time mysterious and beautiful beyond words. I continued to be aware of it for three months and then it faded, but the memory of what it was like has been very important for me.'

Drugs are used also, of course, for other reasons than the expansion of consciousness. Drug-taking as a method of achieving supraliminal awareness intersects with drug-taking as an escape from the pains of life – indeed this is why, in some cases, supraliminal awareness is sought. All too often, then, the desire for illumination and the desire for oblivion are merged in drug-taking, and the result is a deadly addiction, conferring dreams which change to nightmares rather than reveal or inspire visions. Even the apparently benign and delightful marijuana, which soothes the harshness of life for many a villager in the Middle East and elsewhere, can be misused. In many cases the pleasant relaxation and slowing down become such a need that real life can hardly be lived. What should help us to tolerate our difficulties and to act fruitfully because we are refreshed ends, in extreme cases, by preventing all action.

Of course there is much we do not know about the effects of drugs on the human organism. This is one argument against legalizing marijuana, which could turn out to be as malign as tobacco. Moralistic factors further confuse our attitude towards drugs. To a member of a civilization steeped in the Protestant ethic it all seems too easy. There is no price, at least no price in terms of effort, yet we may receive as reward something that is indistinguishable from the Beatific Vision sometimes – but by no means always – granted to great saints after years of meditation, prayer, and mortification. It doesn't seem quite fair. Apart from the unfairness there is another doubt, though I admit that this may be a rationalization of my objection to the quick spiritual fix. I believe that the most important quality of all is awareness. It is a more or less constantly high level of awareness that enables us to achieve a greater measure of autonomy and to act more consistently to eliminate social ills. It seems to me that drug-induced awareness, though potentially valuable and influential, does not actually alter the general level of self-consciousness. It helps us to realize that there are different levels to attain; it does not establish these levels within us. As I suggest later, I believe that this can be accomplished only through constant and serious effort.

Drugs, then, may help us to define goals for which to strive by different means; they may delude us into thinking we have achieved these goals; and they can all too easily dehumanize and destroy us.

(iii) *The Counter-culture Builders*

The counter-culture, so ably defined by Theodore Roszak (1967), is an alternative life-style, an approach to living quite different from, though not necessarily in open conflict with, current conventions. It is, in fact, an objective common to both militants and mystics, who, to the extent that they reject contemporary society, are trying to build, both conceptually and actually, a different model. When one considers their attitudes towards sex, self-realization, money, property, career, 'success', the meaning and value of community, nationhood, and human relationships in general, it is clear that there is as radical a difference today as in any period of history between those who want to change the society of their time and those (often their parents) who, being steeped in belonging-identity, seek to preserve it. Many advocates of the counter-culture are attempting, so far as this is possible, to exemplify their ideals.[14] They live together in communes, earning their living, or in some senses literally making it, with the minimum of compromise with the world of the market. They run their community affairs as well as their interpersonal relationships on principles that are most seriously intended to preserve and increase individual autonomy and to promote the fullest realization of the human spirit. The high seriousness demonstrates the high morality, but it is manifested in a manner that strikes some as evil. It leads, for example, to greater sexual freedom and a rejection of the work ethic, which the square sectors of society, appalled, denounce as being in the highest degree wicked.

It is worth pausing to consider why the counter-culture in all its manifestations – especially the strange appearance of its proponents and their relaxed approach to life – arouses such a violent reaction in so large a segment of the population. It is because they feel threatened. Here, they sense, is another technique of existence which, if more widely accepted, would completely undermine their belonging-identity.

Although all persons who have reached a certain degree of awareness are proponents of the counter-culture, I associate it particularly with the supraliminal aspirants. It is in the communes that the construction of a new sort of society is being most systematically undertaken and it is there that specifically spiritual objectives (through, for example, meditation or yoga) are most constantly pursued. Andrew Rigby,[15] who has carried out an exhaustive study of British communes, maintains that they all have an underlying spiritual purpose. At the same time, many of them are conscious experiments in the establishment of new patterns of governance and association which – after unimaginable upheavals – may eventually replace the established ones.

The militants who are concerned with such issues tend to be more interested in the reshaping of economic and political institutions. They are, so to speak, more objective. The mystics are concerned rather with interpersonal structures which depend directly on the nature of the individuals concerned. This is in many ways a more full-time job. These types of development evolve with the evolution of human beings. It is simpler (if more dangerous) to consider what needs to be done at an intellectual level than to try to bring it about at a practical one.

The counter-culture, as manifested in these self-conscious attempts to create new social forms based on higher awareness of a supraliminal type, blends the objective and the subjective. Without being any less spiritual in its implications it is the most concrete of the modes of supraliminal awareness. The musical show, *Hair*, a fascinating mixture of sex, religion, and high-spirited fun, suggested various aspects of the counter-culture very strongly. The popularity and therefore inevitably the influence of *Hair* show that the first assumption of the counter-culture is correct: it can be spread widely.

What we do not know is how the conflict between what might be termed the culture of the silent majority and the counter-culture will develop. Establishments, as I have noted, already feel threatened. Police and local authorities feel particularly menaced by hippies and communes, long hair and beads, and are happy to find legalistic grounds for hounding the individuals concerned from place to place (their residence permits are improper, their conditions of sanitation do not conform to local standards, etc.). They are given a hard time by immigration and customs officials when they travel. But whether the counter-culture will erode the square culture, or be crushed by it, or continue indefinitely to coexist with it, or lose its spirit and die out, it is hard yet to predict.

(iv) *The Psycho-philosophers*

I apply this term to those who are systematically following a course of self-development in an attempt to increase awareness, and here I mean a fairly specific course based on a demanding rigorous system. The commune members described in the previous section are also trying to raise their awareness level, but they are more often looking for a system than following one. They sense that there are techniques and that these may become apparent if they meditate, read the *Upanishads*, study the *Tibetan Book of the Dead*, practise divination with the *I Ching* (see Blofeld, 1965), and so on. They may or may not be right – the point of interest is that they have chosen, as have so many others, the supraliminal path. However, very few of them are what I would call psycho-philosophers.

The psycho-philosophers are those who follow an existing system, not one they are inventing or trying to extract from esoteric or occult literature. Such are the systems formerly taught by Ouspensky (1949) and Gurdjieff (1963). In the context of our discussion these people are interesting in two particular ways: their approach to human evolution and their connection with social action.

In the view of these systems (and I am really dealing with those I have just referred to – there are others, including various branches of yoga, which I conceive to be similar but of which I know little) men in their ordinary state are both asleep and lacking any central core of personality. They are automata who misuse the machine of tremendous potential with which they are by nature endowed. The first stage of evolution from this state is to recognize it for what it is and to seek ways of remedying it.

This corresponds in a sense to the dawning of awareness, though I use the term more loosely. Subsequent efforts are directed to constructing the real I or self or personality, out of the fractionated potential we possess now. Eventually, as we awaken and become more real, we develop greater autonomy. We are no longer the creatures of every shifting and uncontrollable mood. We begin to use ourselves with a greater economy and power as faculties which have been misused start to operate properly. From the point of view of this book it is irrelevant to go into details of how these changes occur. I need only emphasize that it requires a sustained effort to increase awareness and that one of the prime objectives is to build a real self.

The social commitments of the psycho-philosophers are somewhat different from those of the other groups described. Psycho-philosophers are no less aware of social evils – possibly they are even more aware in this respect since they have a particular view of the forces governing large-scale events and behaviour. And like others who seek supraliminal awareness they feel that there is nothing they can do to influence things *as they are now*, so they seek to change and develop within themselves. What differentiates them is the long-term nature of their goals. They do not envisage a stage in six months or a year or five years when they will be better able to influence, say, their local community. They do not feel able to specify in any particular sense what they might do. Their essential contribution may never be definable save as a subtle change in the psychic chemistry of the world. For this reason the psycho-philosophers are less likely than many others to have programmes of social change or to join communes (though they may set up their own communes) and are more likely to lead outwardly ordinary lives, following their careers and not indulging in sartorial or behavioural extravaganza.

(v) *The Nirvana-seekers*

I contrast the psycho-philosophers with those I term the nirvana-seekers because what they seek is thought by many, I believe wrongly, to be the meaning of nirvana.[16] They are people who believe in the loss or destruction of the personality, in its merging with the absolute, and consequent extinction. Since their beliefs are in a sense a negation of certain aspects of awareness I wonder whether it is even appropriate to include such people here – but I do so because undoubtedly their particular ambience did originate in awareness.

Those who think in these terms appear to me to have suffered a very severe shock in the process of developing awareness. They have for some reason been unable to tolerate what they have perceived within and around themselves, but they are too aware to retreat into the world of belonging. Instead they have taken what might be considered a side-step into a mode of supraliminal thinking which enables them to withdraw both from society and from themselves. I say that they withdraw from themselves because they are striving for a condition sanctioned by some interpretations of some Oriental teachings in which awareness leads to the end of awareness, to oblivion and the end of pain.

I believe that there are many young people, including some of the most sensitive, whose awareness is associated with intolerable anguish and confusion and who become what psychiatry would term schizoid, withdrawing from the world, cutting their ties with others, and rationalizing the ultimate act of personality destruction – which is, of course, the final withdrawal.

At this point I should perhaps restate a previous argument. Some of my friends have objected that a diminution of belonging-identity is in itself schizoid and likely to lead to severe disturbance. But the sense of belonging as it relates to family, community, associates, humanity, is primarily significant in that it helps one to define one's own identity. Only secondarily does one act positively towards people one belongs to (or vice versa) *because it strengthens the belonging*. It is very possible, however, to have warm and positive relationships of commitment, concern, and love with people outside the context of belonging. Indeed I would maintain that the best relationships, in which we genuinely care more for the good of the other than for ourselves, must be outside the dependency of belonging. Moreover, awareness, as I have indicated, implies awareness of others; it implies that we see them in their own right and not as agents to increase or decrease the security of our identity. The nirvana-seekers have, I believe, taken a wrong turn.

(vi) *The Hippies*

Naturally a number of those we have already discussed under other categories might be termed hippies. No matter. The categories combine and overlap. I use the word specifically as a kind of catch-all for those gentle, loving people who are not militant by temperament, who have not joined a particular movement, spiritual, ideological, or social, but who want to lead their own lives harming no one and 'doing their own thing'. There are, of course, false hippies who wear the clothes and speak the jargon but have neither the awareness nor the heart. We need not be concerned with them. But the genuine hippies are sufficiently numerous to constitute, I believe, a significant phenomenon.

There were no hippies in my generation of young people, or, if there were, they wisely kept quiet about it. Most of us had a firm belonging-identity based largely on the traditions of class and school and derided those who failed to conform or were deficient in the proper strengths of belonging. It was almost inconceivable that we should reject all these things and forfeit the great advantages they brought. I am constantly amazed that this generation has achieved, so collectively for all the exceptions, a level of awareness which has enabled it to cast off its belonging-identity and related material assets. I am also impressed by the rich diversity of the hippie type. It is not, of course, necessary to have dropped out to be a hippie – many are still 'in', in the sense that they are working or studying. But they are hippies in their rejection of violence, the anti-human qualities of society, and the belonging-identity, and in their acceptance of love, of caring for each other, and, perhaps, of what the Quakers call 'that of God in every man'.

Tony: a failed militant

Tony is in his mid-twenties. As a student he was very active politically, particularly in opposition to Britain's nuclear policy. He went on many marches, demonstrated in front of 10 Downing

CONFIGURATIONS OF AWARENESS AND IDENTITY II

Street and the American Embassy, was arrested several times, contributed to the radical press, and even stood – unsuccessfully – for Parliament.

Gradually he came to believe not only that his activism was achieving nothing, but that his whole way of life was somehow unfulfilling. Something in him was not being satisfied. He began to see that in certain vital respects he was out of sympathy with most of his associates. Their goals were all objective political ones. Many of them were also, of course, dissatisfied with the quality of life, but this only intensified their efforts: when the institutions had been reformed things would become better.

Tony, however, could not wholeheartedly accept this view. He began to hold with increasing conviction that such efforts were unlikely to effect lasting or desirable alterations in the structure of society. Suppose that the positions of the social classes were simply reversed: would not the old inequities just be perpetuated under another name? A more fundamental transformation was, perhaps, necessary. The culture must be more radically rethought, but for this to happen the aims and attitudes of people must be reordered. Some kind of widening of consciousness would be essential and – as Tony acknowledged with surprise – this seemed to imply the acceptance of some spiritual belief. Just what he meant by this he could not define, but he knew that this new approach went beyond the pragmatic socio-political theories by which he had lived before. The most important aspect of it was that it involved bringing about a change in himself.

Tony, fortunately, was a competent research chemist and during this period of inner questioning he continued to work and to keep himself comfortably. Here he was luckier than those whose crisis in the development of awareness hits them when they are younger, such as students who then give up their studies (and their grants) but have no earning power. He quietly sought out a group of like-minded young people and they set themselves up in adjacent houses in a poor area of London, sharing their ideas and their resources and trying to build a community in which new values were practised. They attempted to get away, so far as is possible, from the normal involvement in the economy and are in fact planning to sell their London property and move into the country, where they will grow their own food and make themselves as independent as they can. Tony has not entirely given up the goals he had as a militant. He now believes that the established order is too strong to be taken by frontal assault; if, however, the alternative mode of living with which he and his friends are beginning to experiment is successful, a surprise attack will have been made from the rear. They hope that the alternative model of society they are offering will draw more and more people away from the competitive materialism of the existing one and so weaken it that it eventually disintegrates.

At the same time, they are trying to prepare themselves for the tasks ahead. They read a great deal of mystical or esoteric literature, they discuss and they meditate communally. Tony is particularly drawn by the ethic of Christian poverty and wants to give up his job, but he keeps on earning for the good of the community until they move out of London.

Priscilla: a drug-taker

Priscilla is the third daughter of parents who doted on her and for some reason favoured her much more than her other siblings. She was not particularly gifted academically, but was so charming, feminine, and attractive that people were won over by her and expected her to do more than she was able. Into the bargain, she was affectionate and sensitive; men and boys fell in love with her in considerable numbers.

She was deeply moved by the horrors of Vietnam and Biafra and indeed by all the inhumanities that taint our existence. She was too gentle for militancy and drifted delightfully through life, writing a little bad poetry, having romantic but short-lived affairs, and failing her examinations. She began, around the age of twenty-one, to feel that something was missing, that there was some perception that might give her the clue to the meaning of life, but was for ever eluding her.

It is not surprising that, like so many others, she took to drugs in the hope that they would supply what was missing.

At first, in a sense, they did. She was only on pot and it gave her a sense of benevolent wellbeing, with occasional revelatory perceptual changes that were very satisfying. But the more she smoked the more she drifted. She dropped out of college, proclaiming to her parents that she had a mission to preach love and that they had a duty to support her. When her father said that he would support her only if she lived at home, she flew into a violent rage and left the same night, having stolen all the available cash and her mother's jewellery.

Nobody now knows where she is or what she is doing. Twice during the last two years she has been seen by people who had known her previously. Once she was pregnant. Both times, judging by her strange manner and her inaccessibility, she was on hard drugs. She spoke harshly and coarsely, reviling her parents, indeed the whole older generation, as capitalist pigs.

The charming, affectionate Priscilla had disappeared.

Roger: a counter-culture builder

Roger is a wood-carver and furniture-maker of great talent. Although he is only in his late twenties, his work is well known and fetches a high price, but he is not interested in making money. He lives very frugally with his wife and baby and devotes most of his time to teaching promising young men and women to work in wood. He charges them nothing because his main purpose is to impart not a technical skill, but an appreciation of wood, a sense of the artist's responsibilities, and a feeling of community among those engaged in the same craft.

Roger is both gay and serious. He has a personality at once complex and harmonious, gentle and firm. He treats his students as equals and indeed feels them to be equally engaged in the same quest, but he has much quiet authority. This derives from the justice, care, skill, and unselfishness with which he approaches everything.

He hopes to be able to establish a community of like-minded

craftsmen artists. They would maintain themselves through their work, but their primary purpose would be to constitute a group of people living together in accordance with certain principles. Their art would be a focusing point for these principles and indeed an expression of them, but Roger's ideas encompass more than that. He believes deeply in what he terms the spiritual unity of man (and rises very early each day to meditate on this) and is seeking for a way of expressing it more fully. He says that he uses the vehicle of carving, since this is the ability with which he has been blessed, but if he had been a musician or a mathematician then music or mathematics would have served as the basis for doing the same thing.

Roger is out of sympathy with the contemporary way of life, but says it is a waste of energy to attack it. It is more important to establish a very different pattern of living. He calls this the affirmative rather than the negative approach. He and Tony see things very similarly, but whereas Tony passed through various vicissitudes before reaching his present viewpoint, Roger has been moving steadfastly in the same direction since he was eighteen.

Martha: a psycho-philosopher

Martha is outwardly, perhaps, the least unusual of the mystics I am describing. She is a Ph.D. student of philology at the University of London, a serious competent scholar who is not at all concerned about the 'irrelevance' of her work. Indeed, she claims that it is highly relevant because a closer understanding of words enables her to comprehend the esoteric writings that interest her. She is not much interested in the current concerns of many other people of higher awareness, and considers activism to be useless. It is not that she is unmoved by the ills of the world; rather, she believes that they are caused primarily by the blindness of man and that to change the institutions he builds in his blindness is only another form of self-delusion. The most important thing, therefore, is to work for an increase of awareness.

She belongs to a particular psycho-philosophical school which demands a great deal of its members. They meet regularly once a week, and at least one week-end a month they go into a sort of retreat on an estate in the country where, under strict discipline, they do hard manual work. They are expected at all times to keep a strict watch on themselves, to eradicate negative emotions, to avoid wasteful activities such as daydreaming and idle talk. They are encouraged to avoid anything that would draw attention to themselves – extravagant talk, exotic dress, showy behaviour – because, at their stage of development, such things would only emphasize trivial aspects of a personality that is neither unified nor autonomous; would merely impede their attempts to build a real I.

In consequence, Martha is rather quiet and reserved and appears to lack spontaneity. She dresses with taste but not ostentatiously. She works hard and, her tutor says, brilliantly. She is a considerate and thoughtful daughter to parents who find it hard to understand her.

Martha joined the school because of some unusual experiences of time. On several occasions an event (one was a car accident) that lasted only seconds seemed to continue for hours. During these times she had an extraordinary sense of the significance of changes in herself which are usually too swift to be perceived. She could feel, as it were, her heart changing gear, messages being passed along the nerves between her brain and her limbs or organs, the surge of adrenalin being pumped into her system, her sweat glands being activated. These sensations made her feel that we may be unaware of many of the most fundamental aspects of our existence. After searching for some time she found a group of people who appeared to have a method that might provide such awareness.

As time passed her objectives broadened. She no longer sought knowledge for herself, but came to believe that the school, including her belonging to it, constituted a vitally important element in existence. The evolution of the members of the school provided a kind of essential spiritual vitamin for the growth of the rest of humanity. She would not enlarge further on her basic objectives, stating that she could not say what, in practical terms, might come as a result of her personal growth. She might simply continue her work in philology, or some other role might, unpredictably, be assigned to her. But however things might be worked out – and she implied a purpose that was out of her hands – she would remain a member of the school.

Bill: a nirvana-seeker

Like Martha, Bill is an excellent student. Like her he is drawn by esoteric teachings, but there the resemblance ends. Not only is he American and a sociologist, but his intellectual and emotional background is completely different. Martha has always been stable, almost staid. Bill was a brilliant, versatile, and impressionable boy, easily hurt, imaginative, volatile. By the time he went to college his sensitivity to suffering and inhumanity was extraordinarily acute. It was as though his psychic nerve-endings were raw and uncovered.

It was all too much for him. He began to withdraw from the situation that caused him such pain and confusion. As happens so often, ironically, in similar circumstances, he withdrew from the loving and tolerant family and friends who might have helped him to cope with life.

Perhaps because of some unconscious need to rationalize what he was doing he went deeper into the study of Eastern religions which had always interested him. Significantly, however, he selected not the teachings that aim to rebuild or perfect man's nature so that he can act in a fashion which is both more autonomous and in greater conformity with some cosmic purpose, but those interpretations of Buddhism which imply that the goal of development is extinction. When Bill meditated, he dwelt constantly on obliteration. He longed for the absorption of his suffering self in a greater whole where he would find oblivion, not being.

In the meantime he continued to exist, an automaton carrying out familiar tasks without either zest or attention, remote from friends and family, still capable of brilliance when intellectually stirred, but increasingly hard to reach. One of his friends, distressed at his schizoid withdrawal, urged him to seek psychiatric help, but he instantly and completely rejected the suggestion.

Mary: a hippie

It may surprise some that I choose Mary as the illustration of my hippie-type. She is always beautifully, if exotically, dressed, she has a clean and cared-for apartment, and she has a job. But she has what I believe to be the basic hippie qualities – which are by no means possessed by many of the ragged, desperate, undernourished, and sick young people who lead both hopeless and disordered lives on the fringe of society. These are the false hippies, the people of low awareness who find in what they feel to be the hippie mode a sanction for their schizoid alienation.

Mary is gentle, affectionate, and artistic. She invests her life with a particular quality of authenticity and sincerity. There is complete consistency about what she does, and what she does has a splendid individuality.

She tries consciously to introduce an element of creative originality into everything, whether it is cooking a new dish, making a dress, decorating a room – her apartment is full of marvellously ingenious and delightful effects produced at very little cost – or building a friendship. She is always giving her friends charming surprises, appropriate little gifts she has picked up cheaply, poems copied out in her beautiful script, and many other expressions of her affectionate concern. She is in fact a good artist and a competent musician, but one feels that her main field of artistry is the whole of life.

She has never been a militant, though she respects and has worked for several activists and shares their fundamental ideas about society. But perhaps her sensibilities are too sensitive. Violence, and indeed any form of cruelty, horrifies her to the point of physical nausea.

Mary is completely outside the bourgeois middle-class society from which she came. Her alienation from her background goes far deeper than rejection of its sexual morality. She has completely turned away from the idea of any society that is not built on the loving concern of its members for each other, on artistic integrity, and on the freedom of individuals to develop to the fullest extent. She has lived out this rejection with a kind of quiet defiance.

However, she has had to pay a price. The strain of creating a different style of life and a new identity, and of separating herself from her roots, has been considerable. As a result, Mary, though in the most profound sense highly courageous in her persistent turning aside from everything that seems to her cruel, ugly, unjust, or limiting, is also an anxious person with some unexpected and even groundless fears. It may be hoped that, as her awareness-identity becomes strengthened, the anxieties will fade.

Jane, Oliver, and Patrick: three mystics who are not easy to type
These three people, two young and one considerably older, do not fit adequately into any of the previous categories. They are, however, of definitely high awareness and, although two of them have been militants in the past (Oliver having been especially active) and are so to some extent today, I would describe them essentially as mystics. This difficulty of categorization applies, of course, to many people. Extreme militants and extreme mystics are probably much less common – as one would expect in any distribution of types – than those who have a considerable amount of both propensities. Jane and Oliver, and to a lesser extent Patrick, are examples of these people.

Jane is a strong and attractive young woman. She worked in community development as a Peace Corps Volunteer in a remote region of Pakistan where she loved the people and was loved by them. On her return home she decided to dedicate herself to this sort of work. As a first step, she spent three years teaching, initially in Alaska and subsequently in a very poor region of Appalachia. Then she enrolled as a doctoral student in what was termed the Social Change Program of a well-known university. During this period she underwent analysis and, in addition, had much experience of T-groups. She is now in Asia, attached to a social welfare agency and working with tribal people.

So far this is the story of a highly motivated and practical girl who, although tolerably radical in her views, was prepared to work through the system. Such a picture gives little idea, however, of the essences that have been maturing in Jane's nature. I remember her as she was when we first met several years ago, a straightforwardly delightful girl with well-formed but somewhat conventional ideals. The ideals have not actually altered, but Jane has, and they in the process have acquired a new dimension.

Jane radiates a kind of reflective tenderness. She has been saddened by the suffering she has seen and, while she continues to fight it, she is greatly discouraged by the human greed and selfishness that have caused it. Although she continues to try to improve the material conditions of the tribe she is working with, she feels that her main purpose is to change the inner attitudes of the people responsible for those conditions – and she accepts her part of the collective responsibility. She agonizes over the incomprehension of those she tries to discuss these things with, and over her own inability to persuade them that what they stand for is wrong. She does not realize that she is developing a standard of evaluation which, in the world's terms, is very rare, and that she herself has very unusual sensibilities.

Oliver was one of the original Berkeley revolutionaries. For a couple of years he was really in the forefront of the youth scene. He organized and led demonstrations and sit-ins, he experimented with drugs, he helped to develop the new style of thought and living. After he graduated he went to Tanzania, where he taught English for a couple of years in a rural secondary school. During this period he got much involved with the politics of Southern Africa. He went to Rhodesia to make contact with some of the resistance groups, but was very soon picked up by the police, interrogated, and expelled.

During all this time, Oliver's intense political preoccupations never quite succeeded in smothering his intellectual ones. When he returned from Africa the latter came into the ascendant. He continued politicking on the side, but devoted most of his time to studying the process of literary creation. He gathered round him a group of young people and they established together a sort of writing school. Their aim was to devise a form of writing that would adequately express the process of growth and decay in the human spirit. In this, Oliver took the lead as easily as he had earlier in Berkeley. His first book of poems was acclaimed by one critic as 'the authentic voice of the soul of the late sixties'.

Oliver denies that he has withdrawn from the world. On the contrary, he affirms that he was formerly on the surface of things, but now has penetrated more deeply into their nature. He is not prepared to guess what he will be led to by his deeper understanding.

Patrick is a business executive who is also a trustee of his local college. He is a middle-aged man of good education, happily married, modestly successful, and – until recently – liberal in a rather conservative way. A few years ago he had a slight bout of middle-age depression and spent two years in therapy. This, he said, was a most enlightening experience which both gave him new insight into himself and eroded his conventional ideas about race, class, and youth.

He became something of an apostle of techniques for widening awareness (as well as something of a bore to his more conventional associates and friends). He is not in favour of drugs, though open about marijuana, but is very keen on T-groups and other types of sensitivity training and has been active in both experiencing and promoting them.

His newly developed awareness has given him great sympathy for young people and he shocks his fellow-trustees by his espousal of their cause. But they fail to see that he discriminates between those who are sincerely concerned about what they feel to be unjust, inhumane, or sham, and those who have jumped onto the bandwagon of protest, whose militancy is entirely negative, and who are simply using tough and often unpleasant tactics to obtain concessions for which they make no return or to satisfy a craving for violence or publicity.

Although Patrick has acquired a considerable amount of self-conscious awareness, which is perhaps more usually associated with militancy, I rate him among the mystics. He sympathizes with the militants and supports them at trustee meetings as strongly as he can, but he is not one himself. He still dresses and behaves soberly and the only observable sign of his altered outlook is a slight lengthening of the sideburns. But otherwise he is very different, his inward eye is open and he sees what he never saw before. Not only does he perceive facets of the human situation that were hidden to him, but the world seems a brighter, more exciting place. One cannot help wondering what will happen to him, and in him, next.

Configuration 4

It is not easy to discuss this configuration. We infer its existence rather than know it directly. There are many examples of the other identity and awareness patterns – indeed, we have known most of them in ourselves – but it is difficult, in some respects impossible, to speak about a level of consciousness we have not ourselves experienced. We simply cannot know what it reveals. People who have had vivid experiences of wider awareness, whether brought about by drugs, meditation, spiritual or psycho-philosophical exercises, illness, or strange circumstances of chance, find it hard to describe them. They refer frequently to light, colours, brightness, warmth; they speak of patterns in which individual and cosmos are joined; they tell of union, ecstasy, the cessation of time, bliss, often using sexual metaphors, such as marriage or union with the beloved, to describe them.[17]

It would, however, be wrong to assume that high awareness must necessarily have a mystical quality or that flashes of supraliminal awareness are more important than a sustained high level of natural awareness. There are people whose harmonious purposefulness would seem to indicate a strong awareness-identity, but who have not had, or at any rate do not refer to, supraliminal experiences. Nevertheless they have a relaxed control over themselves and a degree of objective compassion for others which noticeably differentiate them. It is as hard for us to comprehend what it is that their level of awareness shows as to understand more dramatically strange manifestations. It may, indeed, be harder. Most of us have had supraliminal glimpses, but high natural awareness is a kind of apotheosis of the normal which is perhaps much more unusual.

We lack the vocabulary to describe these states. We cannot say, having neither the words nor the knowledge, what it is like to have a level of awareness of any sort that is sufficiently high to provide the basis of identity. But there are reasons why we can be sure that such a level can be attained.

First, we have all heard of, and many of us have actually met, people whose strength, wisdom, and understanding were so exceptional that their psychic processes seemed to be beyond the range of our comprehension. Among the most explicit of these have been, naturally enough perhaps, great psychologists. In the writings of Freud and Jung, especially the letters of the former (see E. Freud, 1960) and the autobiography of the latter (Jung, 1961), we get a partial insight into the thoughts and inner experiences of two men who struggled purposefully to achieve self-awareness. Both reached a level where it is impossible to follow them: *we cannot imagine what it was like to be them*. I find Jung particularly baffling. Some passages in his autobiography are so strange that were it not known that he was a man of balance and calmness, a noble and well-developed human being capable of brilliant originality and sustained intellectual effort, one might consider him to have been almost insane. Second, our own occasional shafts of insight show us that higher awareness is possible. What we cannot know is what it means to achieve this more consistently. Third, I suppose we can assume that, just as the higher level of awareness of the hippie or the militant student is beyond the comprehension of those with a strong belonging-identity, so there will be still higher levels that are beyond the comprehension of most people.

If, then, there are people whose awareness is much higher on the average than ours and if they define themselves in terms of this awareness, we can infer some things about them. They will be very much in command of themselves. They will not seek popularity or be dependent on the good opinion of others. Their behaviour will be steadfast and consistent, and they will not easily be shaken by doubt or anxiety. Their actions and speech will be governed by their values. These values will be objective, unselfish, and altruistic, of the sort Maslow (1968) calls B-values. Such people will have a clear perception of human and social problems. While deeply committed to the service of humanity, they will be in a sense detached: they will not be deflected by emotions that attack less aware individuals, such as pity which turns to self-pity, anger however righteous, bitterness at wrongs, resentment at injustice. (These are 'natural' feelings which nevertheless damage our capacity to act.) The overriding impression, perhaps, will be that they are whole and autonomous beings.

In considering persons whom I know to possess these qualities, I am struck by the fact that almost every one of them has two other attributes: a non-violent approach to the elimination of social wrongs and injustices, that is of unpeaceful relationships, and deeply held moral beliefs amounting at times to spiritual or even, in a more formal sense, religious convictions. The correlation is so close that I am inclined to consider these attributes as being part of the definition. The non-violence does not seem to me to be hard to explain: no one with profound human awareness can wish to bring advantage to one group at the cost of suffering to another, even if they are the oppressors. Therefore he seeks other techniques of producing change. The frequency of spiritual or religious belief is possibly more puzzling. I would find it hard to credit that any creed, or indeed religions as a whole, had a monopoly of the truth. Nor do I believe that belonging to a church, even if one has strong religious convictions, does much to increase awareness. On the contrary, it may hinder it. Religion can be an opiate that dulls awareness, it can be a tool of belonging, it can impart a deadening spiritual superiority; the majority of people are perhaps affected in these ways. I am inclined to believe that the important part religious practices seem to play in the development of high awareness is due to two things. The first is that almost all religions, whatever the doctrine, encourage meditation, prayer, or other exercises which force the individual to take stock of himself and to come to terms with his own nature so that he can better fulfil some spiritual purpose. These are in fact exercises in awareness which are undertaken all the more seriously if engaged in for some transcendental purpose. Second, virtually all religions emphasize service, in the name of God, to one's fellow-men.

At this stage I should share a logical problem of presentation with the reader. I posit the existence of a type; I maintain that there is very little in our ordinary experience to inform us what it is like to belong to this type; I then list the characteristics by which members of the type may be recognized. Am I simply exploiting my own predictions, inventing a type and endowing it with the qualities I admire? I can only say that there are people of the sort I have described; they are rare, but far from unknown. Moreover, if I am at all correct in my concepts of identity and awareness and the types related to the various configurations, men of high awareness would be expected to be as I have suggested. But I admit that it is impossible to escape all logical problems when one is dealing with things of which one has no direct experience.

There are various counterfeit high-awareness types. One is the 'strong' character whose strength derives from ambition, from a ruthless egocentricity, or from a well-organized belonging-identity. Another is the highly sophisticated intellectual whose arguments are hard to refute and who is apparently wise and well disposed, but who lacks human understanding. A third is what might be called the compulsive humanitarian who is driven more by guilt than by an objective assessment of need but who nevertheless may lead a life of conspicuous service. Fourth, there are the followers of many religious, philosophical, or mystical cults who speak and behave outwardly as though they have reached a level of awareness they have not in fact attained; this is a very common

CONFIGURATIONS OF AWARENESS AND IDENTITY II

fault and I suspect that almost everyone who is interested in these things has committed it.

High-awareness types are also to be differentiated from extreme versions of the militancy or mysticism discussed in preceding sections. From their writings and from what has been written about them I would imagine Frantz Fanon to be an example of the former (see Fanon, 1967) and Timothy Leary an example of the latter (Leary, 1968). Both have been highly influential as leaders, in very different ways, of revolutionary thought, but an angry violence in Fanon and a certain mushy lack of realism about Leary suggest an absence of inner harmony in the first and of disciplined control in the second. Winston Churchill was another influential leader, but his power, by contrast, derived from the very strength of his identity of belonging (specifically to the upper reaches of English civilization) combined with relatively low awareness.

ILLUSTRATIONS

Who, then, are the people in this configuration of high awareness and strong awareness-identity? I list below some men of note who seem to me, from personal knowledge in four cases and by repute in the others, to have the attributes I have identified – and every reader can, of course, make his own list.

Mahatma Gandhi, because the non-violent techniques of satyagraha showed an equal concern for both exploited and exploiters, and because his search for spiritual truth and self-control and his work for social and political reform were completely interwoven (see Gandhi, 1927, and Erikson, 1969).

Alan Paton,[18] because of his political non-violent militancy and his calm, almost affectionate, refusal to yield on moral issues, and because his writings express the whole man.

Julius Nyerere, because he has watchfully avoided the moral and political pitfalls of power, and has forged a practical philosophy for his nation's development based more on the demands of human dignity than on economic growth (see Nyerere, 1967 and 1968).

Pope John XXIII, because his kindly warmth, his loving sympathy, and unselfconscious modesty illuminated the world, and because of the quiet heroism of his death.

Martin Luther King,[19] because his dedicated service to black Americans was uncontaminated by hatred of white ones and because he was completely non-violent in his approach to social change.

Danilo Dolci, because he has devoted his life, at constant risk, to the victims of Mafia oppression in Sicily, and has pursued his purpose with peaceful strength and high moral purpose (see Dolci, 1961).

Akhter Hameed Khan, because his clear vision led him to resign from the prestigious Indian Civil Service and to train himself for an entirely new role in the service of his people, because he combines intellect with dedication and personal majesty, and because he transformed village life in large areas of East Pakistan, now Bangladesh.

Albert Luthuli, because of his unyielding non-violent struggle for justice for his people (see Luthuli, 1962).

I add pen pictures of two people, well known to me and not unknown to the public, though less famous than those mentioned above, whom I believe to belong to this same configuration.

Justin

Justin is a relatively young man who might be called a professional non-violent revolutionary. He has carried out dangerous missions in several combat zones to bring in and organize the distribution of relief supplies to the victims of war. He has taken part in various illegal sit-ins and demonstrations in a number of different countries. On one occasion he spent several short periods in prison for repeatedly committing the same offence, but his persistence eventually led to a re-examination of the case and an alteration of the law. He is engaged on working out the intellectual rationale for a strategy of non-violent but radical social change.

Justin is not the only person to do such things. It is the spirit in which he does them that makes him exceptional. The foundation of his spirit, apparently, is a deep and untroubled religious belief which calls him to action which he believes to be in the service of God but, unlike others who follow such a call, he is illuminated by a spontaneous affection for all the men and women with whom he deals. He is a very happy person, extremely open and relaxed, receptive, reachable, and outgoing. He is married and derives great joy from his family. He is both serious and gay. He makes an immediate impact as an unusually attractive man, complete and self-possessed – which is quite different from the self-assurance that comes from belonging. He has dedicated his life to a course of action which is bound to lead him into increasing conflict with authority. He views this prospect with complete equanimity.

Laura

Like Justin, Laura is exceptionally attractive, though much older than he is. She has a vivid capacity to reach out to people, to accept them whoever they may be for the essence of their being. She is remarkably intelligent and has taught in several universities on topics connected with social change and welfare, but more important is the quiet, competent, and unobtrusive help she gives constantly to family, friends, and countless organizations with which she is concerned. Everyone calls on her and every call is heeded, but she is never swamped by busyness: on the contrary she radiates calm and affection and appears to have as much time as is needed by everyone.

I have never known her intellect or her energies to be dulled by such negative feelings as self-pity, resentment, or vanity. She is a fine wife and mother who has moved through circumstances that would have put a strain on most people with positive and humorous serenity. Finally, she has deep spiritual convictions nourished by prayer and meditation to a point where her whole life seems to be a joyous expression of an inner light.

Laura, like Justin, makes an immediate impression as a complete human being. She inspires absolute trust. Both she and Justin are people with whom one feels one could face almost any emergency.

This tentative and diffident exploration of the configuration of high awareness and strong awareness-identity suggests one extremely interesting thing. At this level mysticism and militancy may be combined. I say 'may' because undoubtedly there are many people of high awareness whose lives are completely private and who make their contribution to humanity in different ways, perhaps simply through the atmosphere of strength and peace with which they are surrounded, or even more subtly. Having met one or two of them I acknowledge their existence with gratitude, but this response to the ills of the world is, so to speak, indirect. I have therefore concentrated, and find it much easier to do so, on those whose awareness, usually related to religious practices and to that extent supraliminal, has led them to militancy.

The combination of mystic and militant is perhaps a manifestation of the wholeness, the unity, that self-knowledge is traditionally reputed to impart. The contradictions are resolved: the inner and the outer, the Yin and the Yang, the light and the dark, no longer cancel each other out but complement and fulfil each other.

In concluding these two chapters which have dealt with various configurations of identity and awareness, I should raise a question which, with some embarrassment, I ask myself while writing. Like many who may read these pages, I expect, I do not quite correspond to any of the types I have described. There must be a number of people who, like me, would not claim to have a very high rating on the awareness scale, who are generally concerned about the great social issues of the day but are not particularly militant, who are to some extent worried about their personal evolution but are not especially mystical. We are the middle men, semi-engaged and semi-mystical. Where do we stand on the scale I have elaborated? We are not, most of us, political extremists in either the militant or the mystical mode. Does this mean that we are more, or less, likely to reach a high level of awareness? I do not know the answer. From one point of view it might seem that excessive development in one direction makes it harder to effect the eventual synthesis of both modes. On the other hand, it is possible that we go furthest by commitment to a particular configuration. Paul of Tarsus, for example, was, according to the standards of his times, a tough, extrovert militant. On the road to Damascus he also acquired supraliminal awareness. But the two styles supplemented rather than diminished each other. He remained a militant, though his objectives were changed, and his new mysticism reinforced his militancy. There is a great deal that we do not know.

6 Changing Awareness Levels

Level of awareness is a key element in life. When awareness is low it is associated with the belonging-identity, which is the source of competitive materialism and all the bitterness and violence that flow therefrom. When it is higher it generates attempts to change the situation through the militant or mystic mode and, ultimately, through a fusion of both. It is important, therefore, to consider how the levels are altered.

AWARENESS-REDUCING AGENTS

We can daily watch the lowering of our own level of awareness. We can see the obliteration of those moments of relatively high self-consciousness, calmness, self-observation, detachment; moments when we have a feeling of strength and wholeness, a clear, warm, and objective view of others. Or rather, we ought to be able to watch this process of change, but the elements involved in it take away our capacity to perceive ourselves objectively. Without realizing it we are suddenly different. How did it happen? Can it be prevented?

Much can no doubt be explained in terms of neurology and psychopathology. The shifting patterns of cortical activity touch associations of anxiety or guilt, with the result that a different, negative feeling seeps into the central position, dominating our mood. Freud's *Psychopathology of Everyday Life* (1901) demonstrates both lucidly and entertainingly how all-pervasive are such mechanisms, how unaware we are of them, and what wide ramifications they have in the psychic structure.

If these relatively benign manifestations of psychopathology can distort memory, speech, and feeling, the clinically more serious ones will have a far greater impact on awareness. Severe anxiety conditions, depressions, paranoid feelings, and the like are prolongations and intensifications of the negative emotional states which, in the experience of us all, temporarily reduce awareness to almost nothing. In these cases the first need is psychotherapy, which imparts to the individual some insight into his condition and thus to some extent raises awareness.

I am concerned, however, not so much with clinically pathological states as with awareness-reducing elements in everyday life. Even those who, by psychiatric standards, have the best mental health are susceptible to these. They are the minor fears and anxieties that plague us all: the pomps and prides with which we hedge our self-doubt; envy; resentment of the success of others; self-pity; the urge to show ourselves (to ourselves and to others) in the most flattering light; peevishness; jealousy; self-indulgent laziness; depression; anger. This sounds like a list of deadly sins and indeed, apart from any theological implications, they are responsible for damaging the awareness on which our ultimate human usefulness depends.

It is interesting that many of these feelings are associated with the belonging-identity. Pride and vanity, for example, build up the self-image. Resentment, jealousy, envy, and anxiety are responses to a threat to the identity. Depression and self-pity result from injury to it. It is, of course, perfectly possible to experience pity (not self-pity) or anger or grief in an objective sense. What might be called 'pure' emotions, that is to say, those that are not servants of identity but are aroused by suffering, or by corruption or exploitation, feel very different. They are strengthening rather than weakening. Unfortunately, even the purest emotions can easily become negative. We may be genuinely sorry at a friend's misfortune, but imperceptibly the clarity of the emotion is clouded: we feel smug that it did not happen to us; or anxiously self-pitying lest it might; or proud self-satisfaction that we feel so keenly for another's hurt.

It is not at all easy to control these shifts. The principal reason is that they erase the awareness that would signal us to try to do so. Thus they either creep upon us so quietly that we do not recognize what is happening, or they take us by storm, as when we are 'carried away' by 'blind rage' which makes us 'beside ourselves'. These common terms significantly illustrate the effects of negative emotions on awareness and autonomy. We are not, however, completely impotent. Even when 'transported' by violent feeling we can sometimes remember who we are and what we are doing and make a purposeful effort to change the direction of our feelings. Old wives' advice is that we should count a hundred, look in the mirror, or hold our breath when in the grip of strong negative emotion. The main point of such procedures (though breath regulation may effect some helpful change in body chemistry) is to stop the automatic sequence of feeling, to effect a pause in which self-observation can be practised.

One great difficulty is, however, that we enjoy our negative emotions. If we are feeling sorry for ourselves we do not want to stop. If we are angry we do not want to be assuaged. When we are not in the grip of these feelings it is hard for us to remember how absorbing they were. It is as though we *become* our emotion; we personify – as it is said – self-satisfaction, greed, jealousy, or whatever it may be. We do not want to abandon what has become our temporary self.

A vicious circle revolves here. To oppose negative emotions with awareness demands an effort of a particular kind; but negative emotions weaken the capacity to make the effort. Indeed, they enervate us generally. Who has not felt 'shaky' after an outburst of anger, or physically debilitated during a fit of depression.

In general, then, people who are being constantly affected by negative emotions – and some are clearly more susceptible than others to anxiety or depression, for example – must find it difficult to generate the strength either to work on themselves or indeed to do many other things requiring sustained or creative effort. On the other hand, people who are not constantly drained by negative emotions should have, as both cause and effect, a higher awareness and a recognizable energy which enable them to deal effectively with their lives and their work.

Thus, in the terms of my schema, level of awareness is particularly threatened in two situations.

The first is when our awareness is relatively low, and our belonging-identity is jeopardized. We then spring to its defence with all the weapons at our disposal. Say, for example, that I am a fairly liberal and tolerant white man whose identity is largely built up through my position in the community. This position and the very nature of the community are then threatened with change by the introduction of a group of coloured immigrants. My liberal ideas are rapidly flushed away. I become extremely hostile to the newcomers, not only because they disturb the pattern of my belonging-identity, but also because *by placing myself in polar opposition to them I am helping to define and reinforce that identity*. My awareness has diminished because I unthinkingly abandon my principles and resort to any intellectual trick to rationalize my fear and hostility.

The second situation occurs at various points along the line of rising awareness and weakening belonging-identity. At this stage it frequently happens that anxiety caused by separation from the specious security of belonging clouds awareness. Indeed, the configuration higher awareness/weak identity is unstable for this reason. It is only when the autonomy of awareness-identity is achieved that belonging-identity ceases to influence us, and to have extreme attraction when we are for whatever reason made to feel uneasy or insecure. In most people, of course, the level of awareness fluctuates, but for some people the pressures are such that the capacity for higher awareness they have previously manifested is more or less permanently dulled. We then meet people who continue to behave like militants or mystics, but who have lost awareness of those roles as techniques of change. Their activities have been subtly transformed into foci of belonging – to the commune, to the movement, to the revolutionary group, to the hippie culture, and so on. Many people continue to play parts although they are no longer aware of their fundamental purpose. These are the real zombies.

WAYS OF RAISING AWARENESS

Up to a certain point, by nature or circumstances, we may be endowed with a higher than average capacity for awareness. This, so to speak, is given. But to raise it beyond this level requires a deliberate effort, and various types of effort can be made.

The method with which we are most familiar, perhaps, is to undergo some kind of psychotherapy. The first step here is to acknowledge that we need therapy. Many people who are sick by accepted clinical standards resist this knowledge. They reject the idea of treatment because to accept it would either damage their self-esteem – it is still easier to accept the need for an appendicectomy than for psychoanalysis – or expose them more closely to sides of their nature they would prefer to keep in the background of consciousness. The admission that we are in need of treatment implies some degree of self-insight, but it may merely be that we are aware of being troubled by a symptom. There is hope, however, that during the course of therapy a more general awareness will develop, but unless it becomes what I have termed self-conscious awareness, little more may be achieved than the unravelling of a minor psychic knot.

Awareness may also be raised by completely fortuitous circumstances. We may be thrust into situations which, so to speak, jolt us awake. I often advise my students, who, being young, lack material commitments and are in a good position to take chances, to visit strange places, do unusual things, throw themselves into movements, take risks. To experience danger, the suffering of others, hardships, the challenge of extraordinary conditions, may draw the scales from our inner eyes. Being forced to take a new sort of heed of what lies around us, we also become more aware of ourselves. By our response to these circumstances we become conscious of new sides of our own nature. But this is a chancy, haphazard business and can hardly be recommended as a systematic approach to the raising of awareness levels.

The essential incentive is a realization that one is deficient in awareness, not that one has a psychological problem as such or that one wants a more exciting life. Most of us, most of the time, have no such thoughts, and the older we grow the less we have them. But occasionally, in middle age, we have the sense of standing at the edge of a mystery, of almost grasping something very important, but being held back by some lack of capacity within ourselves to perceive.

Young people today, being more perceptive than those of my generation, are more aware, if this is not a contradiction, of deficiencies in their awareness. They are prone to blame these deficiencies on certain facets of contemporary civilization, in particular competitive materialism, which not only promotes a lust of belonging but in a sense technologizes everything – including the human spirit. They are of course right, but other ages have had their particular faults. What is constant is the magnetic attraction and the easiness of belonging-identity, coupled with the difficulty of achieving higher awareness. Nevertheless, though today's young people may perhaps exonerate themselves too much, they do recognize the vital necessity for awareness.

Many of the ways by which they seek it are, seemingly, dead ends. For instance, there are innumerable small cults and groups, completely without guidance, which are likely to lead only to disillusion and to a giving up of the search for higher awareness. They are particularly likely to fail when they are attempting, as most of them are, to reach awareness of a supraliminal kind. One reason for this is that the ideas they employ are mainly Oriental, and are thus not only very alien to Western civilization but were intended to be applied or elaborated in special circumstances, such as the relationship of pupil to master. Unfortunately, we have few genuine gurus.

Far more successful, but in a sense more limited, in my experience, are attempts to achieve self-conscious awareness through T-groups, sensitivity training, and the work of organizations such as the Esalen Institute.[20] These are largely based on the group therapy techniques devised by Bion (1961) and others in the 1940s and have an acceptable foundation of well-tried method and concept, but many of them have made a creative and imaginative leap forwards to a point where there is a fusion of science, art, and warm human feelings. Some have leapt too far into absurdity and meaninglessness, but this is only to be expected. However, many people have been helped by them to make a genuine advance in awareness. This is what one T-group participant said:

> 'It was quite extraordinary how conscious I became both of myself and of others. At first, there we all were, locked in our little boxes and really terrified that someone might have the key to open us up. Faced with all these strange people in this extraordinary situation in which none of us had a clue as to what was expected of us, of what we were supposed to do, I got into a sort of panic and wished I had never come. But by the end of the workshop, only ten days, the most amazing change had taken place in, I think, about all of us. Just because we couldn't act out the parts we had learnt to play [note that what he is mainly talking about here is escaping from the belonging-identity] we all began to be very much more ourselves, whatever that means. We weren't a lot of dummies trying to one-up each other; we were human beings engaged in a common effort to be aware of each other and ourselves. It was so difficult, painful and, yes, frightening, to start with. It was so rewarding at the end – we all loved each other. I felt these were some of the very few real relationships I'd had in my life: as the barriers came down in myself and I saw myself as I had never done before, so the barriers came down between me and the others.'

Accounts like this, and there are many of them, are encouraging. But what next? Is high awareness a quality which, once achieved, will persist and perhaps even grow? I tend to think that it is like many garden flowers which, if left to seed themselves, gradually revert to something like the wild state. Awareness needs cultivation. The forces counteracting awareness – belonging-identity, the stress of separation from it, the enervation of negative emotions, apathy – are so strong that unless we struggle to maintain it we, too, will revert. This, of course, applies to all, irrespective of their individual approaches to awareness of different sorts.

I am convinced that the key factor in striving and continuing to strive for awareness is the recognition of how little we have, of how much this impairs our capacities, and of the extent of the damage done by the collective low awareness of the world. We resist this realization emotionally even if we admit it intellectually, but it is not until we are forced to acknowledge it fully that we can begin to accept the arduous work that is involved in raising awareness. Our resistance stems from a combination of laziness and a refusal to admit that we are less autonomous than we would like to think. Sometimes we are impelled to act only when faced with the disastrous effects of our low awareness: a friend is hurt because of our uncontrolled impulse to speak cruelly, or because of a damaging habit we cannot abandon; a job is lost through our inability to concentrate. Sometimes it is the cumulative impact of many minor evidences of our low awareness that makes us want to do better. A simple experiment will demonstrate the low level of our awareness and reinforce our determination to raise it. Let us try to empty our minds of thought for a minute; we will be lucky if we have enough control to prevent stray ideas from sliding into consciousness after less than half that time. I am reminded of a story about Saint Francis. He was journeying with his donkey and entered into a discussion with a fellow-traveller about concentration and prayer. Saint Francis maintained that it was hard; the other, that it was easy. Saint Francis then said that if this man could recite the Lord's Prayer with complete attention, he would give him his donkey. The Saint's companion laughed. 'The donkey is as good as mine', he said, and began to recite, 'Our Father, Who art in Heaven, Thy Kingdom come, Thy Will be done on earth as it is in Heaven – and will you give me the saddle as well?'

Two points should be emphasized about efforts to raise awareness: namely, that they require both self-discipline and the help of others.

Unless we work on ourselves regularly we will achieve little and will gradually backslide into inactivity. Most religions are, in basic purpose, though seldom as practised or understood by most of their adherents, systems for raising awareness; most of them advocate regular observances such as weekly churchgoing and evening prayers. Even such completely non-spiritual practices as eating fish on Fridays (who would not prefer lobster or salmon to the average meat dish?) serve as *aides-mémoire* to remind us of our religious obligations.

Second, it is very hard to be disciplined on our own. There are bound to be occasions when we are lazy, tired, or preoccupied, and it becomes progressively easier for us to forget ourselves. But the companionship of like-minded people makes things better. If one has a fit of lassitude, the others will spur one on. Moreover, joining with others is helpful in itself, as most religions have indicated by their emphasis on communal worship, and as sensitivity training demonstrates in another context.

There are many channels to higher awareness and certainly I would not wish to recommend any single system or non-system more than another. The important thing is that it should be followed seriously but without fanatical exclusiveness. I have known people of many faiths and many kinds of lack of faith who have achieved high awareness, because the question of awareness underlies all major religions and psycho-philosophical systems.

Another way in which we are helped to maintain a higher level of awareness may be mentioned. This is that, as we struggle towards increased awareness, we distil values from our deeper perceptions. These we objectify as specific goals, moral, philosophical, or social, which persist even though our awareness may fluctuate downwards. They remain then like pitons thrust into the rocks of uncertainty by which we may draw ourselves upwards again.

But however we set about raising the level of our awareness, there is one essential thing: *we must at all times try to remember who we are*. This is the fundamental exercise in awareness. We must look at ourselves, feel ourselves as we act in various ways, or talk, or move, or even think. We must try to see ourselves as part of a network of human beings who comprise our family, our friends, community, associates; we must, in a sense, locate ourselves in the universe.

As with most things, of course, it is infinitely easier to say what needs to be done than to do it. It is true that there are a few tricks that may help: it even contributes to awareness to say one's name

('I am Adam Curle') and try to recognize the fact, or to look in a mirror and realize that this is I. We soon find, however, that it is incredibly hard to persist in such efforts. It is almost as though they were impeded by a perverse natural force. This may in a sense be true: for awareness can bring pain and uncertainty, impelling us to make uncomfortable changes in our life. I suspect, though, that there is another and more deep-seated reason. The psychological pressures of existence militate against awareness: they drive us to identify with the things, situations, and emotions that blind us to an objective appreciation of ourselves. We become too easily involved with our anger or fear, caught up in our hopes, absorbed in our interests. We become these things and, however good, altruistic, or creative they may be, in doing so we lose ourselves.

To gain awareness is like swimming upstream. It is intensely hard work and if we relax for a moment we are swept backwards to a point below where we started. Such systems as Zen, the various forms of yoga, sufi practice, and some aspects of Christian mysticism are all directed to achieving increasing awareness. But apparently they all demand enormous efforts with no guarantee of success; the world has a large number of what might be termed failed mystics. For this reason we should perhaps approach the problem of awareness with greater relaxation and receptivity. Intense effort can defeat its own end. If we can point ourselves in the direction of what we perceive as the good, and accept thankfully what happens, we may come nearer to awareness than if we strive grimly to achieve it.

What this further awareness, if cultivated, will eventually reveal can in no way be specified.

In conclusion, it is hard to become aware and many catastrophes can occur on the way. But nevertheless I am not completely pessimistic. Throughout the world, it seems to me, there has taken place in the last quarter of a century an extraordinary awakening of awareness, almost a revolution of awareness.[21] I noticed this first in the Third World. Then it seemed to spread (at least in my limited experience) to the young, especially the educated young, of America and Europe, and to the black people of the USA. I am astonished that so many men and women less than half my age have an awareness of themselves and the world which is so much sharper than mine and of a completely different order from that which I had at their age. Admittedly, many fall by the wayside, for the pressures are great, but I cannot help feeling that, even so, something very remarkable is happening. I may be wrong about the generality of this awakening, but, if I am not, is it too fanciful to suggest that humanity is reacting to the appalling dangers to which we have been brought by materialistic greed and rapacity? Have we perhaps responded to our critical situation by producing a new psychic mutation?

It may in fact be that our awareness of the need to change was stimulated by the very changes against which we are reacting – the extraordinarily rapid changes wrought by technological developments. These have not only incited man's cupidity, thus intensifying injustices and dangers to liberty, but have shaken the foundations of his belief. When the blinkers of traditionalism are removed, letting in a glimpse of a new vision, man can more readily tolerate the confusions and ambiguities that must simultaneously arise; or he can reject them all the more violently and fiercely because the old assurances are partly gone. The greater the volume of awareness, therefore, the greater the probable opposition to it.

7 Makers of Peace and Violence

The conclusions I reach in this chapter will not come as a surprise to the reader. Although the core of this book, everything since Chapter 1, has been devoted to elaborating a system, the implications of that system for my original purpose – if I have expressed myself with any clarity – must be obvious. In the first chapter I defined the processes of peacemaking and placed some emphasis on what I called the revolutionary stages by which the underdog in an unpeaceful relationship achieves, or is helped to achieve, equality with the top dog. These are the stages I termed education and confrontation: unpeaceful relationships of inequality and injustice, which are to be changed by them, are far more prevalent than any others.

Moreover, it is on this sort of unpeaceful relationship that the awareness of today's younger generation, and of a growing number of their elders, is focused. Dissent from and protest against the exploitative network and the spirit of competitive materialism are everywhere evident. The world's students have, as it were almost overnight, become a political force to be taken into account. They have shaken many governments and toppled some – for example, in South Korea and Turkey; they almost succeeded in France. At the same time they are active in the social field, and service to the poorer or underprivileged communities is as much a part of the scene, though less salient, as political work. The political and economic thinking of the New Left, disorganized as it still is, exemplifies this group at an intellectual level. Then again, concern over (or desperation about) the state of affairs has driven many away from involvement in the social system and into communes aimed at establishing the counter-culture, or into various forms of mysticism.

The people concerned, both the militants and the mystics

(except for the various counterfeits I have mentioned), are in Configuration 3, characterized by higher awareness and weak identity (both modes). Their instability, their difficulties, failures, and backslidings – especially as they grow older – stem from their weak identity; and this is the corollary of their higher awareness, which has largely invalidated their earlier belonging-identity. It is probably true to say that unless, by the time they are established in their careers, they have built a much stronger awareness-identity, they will mostly revert to a belonging-identity, with concomitantly lower awareness.

Those whom they oppose, whose opinions they want to change, whose way of living they challenge, whose hold over the poor (when they are rich) they hope to break, or whose acceptance or even ignorance of that hold (when they are poor) they try to shake, are men and women in Configuration 2 (low awareness/strong belonging-identity). There is a mass of stability, inertia, and resistance to significant changes in this group. Despite much instability round the edges where it merges with Configuration 1 (people of low awareness and weak identity) and Configuration 3 (those beginning to be troubled by awakening awareness), the core is almost immovable. There is too much vested interest, emotional and material, in the *status quo*, and the two reinforce each other. I should re-emphasize that these people are no more the wealthy than the impoverished. Both equally resist any threat to their identity with ridicule, anger, and violence. Remember the attack by 'hard hat' construction workers on marchers protesting against the American invasion of Cambodia.[22] This resulted from long pent-up anger against the types of people who, they had been led to believe, were undermining the 'American way of life'.

Let me dwell on this case for a minute: it is complex and illustrative. The construction workers are, as a group, neither particularly well off nor very poor. Their version of the American way of life cannot be very lavish. Like most other workers in a capitalist society they have plenty to complain of, particularly the lack of equality. But they love their chains. They do not see that the American dream of golden opportunity for all has faded and that they are stuck where they are. Are they not all now members of the middle class? Resentments and fears they have, of course, about losing their jobs, about sickness and doctors' bills, about not being able to keep up the payments on the colour TV. But when things go wrong, it's not the system, it's not America that is at fault. To admit that would be dangerous to their identity. It's the long-haired students, the blacks, the commies: apart from them everything would be fine. So, when they have an excuse to bash them, all their anger boils up and they bash them good. They'll feel better afterwards, their identity will be strengthened and confirmed, and the conservatives will be reinforced – except for a few waverers on the fringe who will be alienated by their brutality.

One of the war cries of low awareness/strong belonging-identity is for law and order, and it would be hard to complain of this if law and order did not, in effect, mean – very often – going far beyond what was either legal or orderly in order to suppress groups working for radical reform, and thus ensuring further violent confrontations in the future. Nor should it be taken to mean that people within this configuration are all good, law-abiding citizens. The majority, I suppose, are. But a strong belonging-identity in no way precludes crime. The court records are full of cases in which the criminals were excellent members of their communities, displayed the flag on all appropriate occasions, hated those they considered their country's enemies, and manifested other hallmarks of this configuration – but also embezzled, accepted bribes, practised fraudulent conversion, and were vicious and violent.

These are the opponents of the peacemakers and they are both powerful and, when challenged, ruthless. The peacemakers are, of course, strengthened, indeed inspired, by a higher level of awareness, but they are weakened and rendered unstable by their deficient sense of identity. It is only when awareness is raised to the point where awareness-identity emerges that real stability is established. It is my fear, however, that awareness-identity is something that comes with age. I know few of the young who have come near, so far as I can judge, to achieving it fully, and none of the very young, however sensitive their awareness. The danger is that, before they can develop a stable awareness-identity, their anxieties will have impelled them to revert to the belonging system. The hope is in numbers. The more aware young people there are, the more they will together be able to withstand the formidable pressures upon them.

The other peacemaking techniques, conciliation, bargaining, and development, are applied outside a revolutionary situation when two more or less equal parties to a conflict are reconciled to the point where they can discuss, and with luck resolve, the conflict of interest between them, and finally move forward together in a positive relationship from which each derives benefit.

The situations that require these methods range from the interpersonal (in which the services of, say, a marriage guidance counsellor might be most useful) to the international (where a mediator appointed by the United Nations might be necessary). Every mature human being is, of course, called upon in the course of his ordinary life to act on countless occasions in roles equivalent to those of conciliator, bargainer, and developer, usually in unpeaceful situations involving family members, friends, neighbours, work associates, and so on. But for many interpersonal problems, and many conflict situations involving larger groups or nations, a professional is called for. The conciliator or bargainer will be, for example, a social worker, a psychiatrist, a lawyer practised in mediation, a professional diplomat, an international civil servant. Those concerned with development (that is, with establishing a collaborative relationship and a form of society that makes such collaboration possible and fruitful) will be specialists from a wide range of fields, such as city planners, social workers, lawyers, politicians and political scientists, economists, and educationists. How, if at all, do the people carrying out these jobs fit into the categories we have discussed?

In the first place, these are not revolutionary tasks as such: development in particular is evolutionary. Second, the emphasis is on technology rather than ideology. Third, the work tends to demand people with fairly advanced professional qualifications.

I find myself asking, then, whether there is a complete break in type between the first revolutionary group of people engaged in changing unpeaceful relationships, and the second group who are concerned with the later stages of peacemaking.

My own opinion is that there may be, but that if this is so it is undesirable and could simply lead to a recrudescence of the old unpeaceful relationships. The effective third-party mediator, whether his role is primarily that of conciliator or bargainer, must have, in addition to his professional qualifications, a sensitive awareness of the people on both sides: he must be aware of the strains they are undergoing and the distortions that desperation has wrought on their perceptions, and must have a capacity to understand what they are trying to express even though they are prevented from saying it openly for fear of losing face. He must be able to avoid being sucked into the vortex of strong feelings and thus losing his impartiality, his genuine sympathy for the agonies of both sides, his clear consciousness of the actors and the situations. Unless he is able to do this he will be ineffective. Either he will not contribute to the reaching of a settlement, or – worse – he will be instrumental in fabricating one that is unjust to one or other of the parties.

The tasks of development similarly demand a high level of awareness as well as professional competence. This is vital if the errors of the past are to be prevented, if we are not to slide back into the materialistic rivalries, the chauvinism (that epitome of belonging), the inequalities, the feudal relationships of the past which in fact spawned the conflict.

Thus men and women of high awareness are essential at every stage in the building and maintenance of a peaceful society. The difference between those who practise the skills of revolutionary peacemaking and the others may lie, therefore, not so much in level of awareness and mode of perception of society, as in professional specialization and competence and, probably, age. I am not inferring that the younger activists lack training – many are highly qualified – but their lack of seniority and of extensive practical experience may make them less appropriate for some of the tasks of conciliation, bargaining, and development. (Not that age and experience always count: it is more that people think they do.) It is at these stages, perhaps, that people of my age-group come in – though I hasten to add that this should not preclude us from playing a more militant part should occasion arise.

In *Making Peace* I noted that we live in a most complex web of relationships, large scale and small scale, peaceful and at all stages of unpeacefulness. The scope of peacemaking is unlimited and the contexts within which it can be carried out are immensely various. Some demand opposition to evil and inhuman establishments. Others, particularly those that are primarily developmental, require work within systems. We must be always aware of the multiplicity of tasks and the variety of ways by which they may be tackled.

Awareness and awareness-identity are in eternal conflict, in us and around us, with belonging-identity. Awareness is uncomfortable and insecure. It takes away the pleasant certainties of life, the fixed values, the easy answers to insoluble questions. It pricks the sluggish conscience, inducing us to take a stand when we would prefer to go happily with the herd. It even drives us to undignified and anonymous death for lost causes. It makes us dissatisfied with our lives: our achievements turn sour, and our possessions and position, once highly treasured, are as ashes in our mouths. We fight the implications of awareness. We envy those with what is called 'simple faith' whether it be in God, or country, or a way of life. How lucky they are – in a sense.

Those whose awareness is high are a constant threat to people whose security depends on a belonging-identity. They threaten either to make them, too, feel uncomfortable and dissatisfied, or actually to disrupt their protective systems of belonging. Throughout history the aware have been ridiculed, disowned, hated, tortured, and killed by those who feared them. The persecution and crucifixion of Jesus is just one example. But they are hated so much precisely because they are also attractive. Few people are so blind that they do not feel the compelling force of awareness and with part of their hearts yearn for it. Thus our attacks on the more aware are violent because contact with awareness has aroused doubts in ourselves. We hate those who force us to question ourselves and we escape from having to answer by attacking. We project our inner struggle outwards and many suffer or die or kill because we will not acknowledge our blindness, or try to regain our sight.

NOTES

1. For example: in 1940 infant mortality among non-white Americans was 12·5 per cent higher than among white Americans. In 1965 it was 9·3 per cent higher, but the maternal mortality rate, four times as high for non-whites as for whites, was relatively higher than it was in 1940. In 1965 life-expectancy for whites was 6·9 years longer than for non-whites; and, at the age of 25, life-expectancy for non-whites is 11 years shorter than for whites (National Advisory Commission on Civil Disorders, 1968, pp. 270–2). There is no suggestion that the greater mortality is due to genetic weakness (this possibility is examined and dismissed by Myrdal, 1944, pp. 140–4). Myrdal records that in the late 1930s registered infant mortality for Negroes was 96 per cent higher than for whites, and that this was probably an underestimation.

   One way in which the socio-economic handicaps of black Americans are demonstrated is in evidence that, for blacks, a relatively high level of occupation attained by the father is not often reflected in the son's employment. A government document shows that whereas a majority of the sons of white white-collar workers are employed at the same level as their fathers, this applies to only 10 per cent of the sons of black white-collar workers (US Department of Health, Education and Welfare, 1969, p. 24).

2. Galtung (1969a and 1969b) develops the concept of structural violence to describe this sort of unpeaceful relationship. Violence by neglect and apathy is also termed 'soft violence'.

3. Many of the former French colonies, for example, are too small and too lacking in resources to enjoy the possibility of autonomous economic development. They depend greatly on the former metropolitan power, but they pay a heavy price. They provide cheap raw materials and a captive market for French goods. Worst of all, they are compelled to political subservience. If they should try to break away, as Guinea did with almost disastrous results, they would forfeit French aid and founder economically. As it is, the aid enables them only to survive – not to prosper. See Dumont (1966) for other examples relating to Africa. Gough (1967) maintains that in the fifteen years before her paper was written, 227 million people in sixteen nations moved back into the status of clients of the rich nations, thus joining the majority of their fellows in the Third World.

4. The Tanzanian economic and political philosophy is set out in Nyerere (1967 and 1968), and in *The Arusha Declaration* (1967). Tanzania suffered, like Guinea, for pursuing an independent course of action because Britain cut off all aid. Aid was, however, subsequently restored.

NOTES

5. Power can be thought of as the capacity – moral, political, economic, or military, or any combination of these – to make the other fellow think twice.
6. See the bibliography for works by these authorities.
7. At least when some form of depth psychology is employed. Thus writes Thomas Szasz (1965): 'Psychoanalytic treatment is characterized by its aim – to increase the patient's knowledge of himself and others and hence his freedom of choice in the conduct of his life.'
8. Pascal's 'night of fire' took place from half past ten until half past midnight on 23 November 1654. In many respects it marked a turning-point in his life and, to remind himself of the occasion, he sewed into his lapel a piece of parchment inscribed with the date, the hours of the experience he described as fire, and an invocation. The whole text is reproduced in some editions of his works as pensée 913.
9. See, among their many works, Glueck & Glueck (1959).
10. The views of this great humanitarian are expounded in Pire (1967).
11. Che Guevara's humanity is demonstrated very warmly in Guevara (1967).
12. A young Quaker non-violent revolutionary. See Lakey (1969).
13. These are characterized by the mindless violence and personal disturbance typical of persons, such as Gwenneth, in the low awareness/weak identity configuration.
14. In England, and perhaps elsewhere, they actually have a publication, *Communes: Journal of the Commune Movement*, with a small but rapidly growing circulation.
15. I have had a number of helpful discussions with Mr Rigby.
16. Nirvana, so far as I can comprehend it, is a condition of awakening from illusion. It has a quality of voidness, but this is because of the absence of illusion. It is described in such terms as shining, the unveiling of reality, the state of tone awakening. This may well be incomprehensible, but it does not seem to imply obliteration (see Evans-Wentz, 1954, pp. 1–7).
17. See, for example, James (1902).
18. The spirit, social outlook, and literary artistry of Alan Paton are exemplified in Paton (1944) as well as in his other works not mentioned in the bibliography.
19. For a good account of this great man see King (1969).
20. Described in Schutz (1967).
21. Since I first drafted this passage I have read the work of Reich (1970) which, I found to my gratification, came by a different route to approximately the same conclusions.
22. This is interestingly reported and discussed by Andy Logan in 'Around City Hall', *New Yorker*, 6 June 1970.

Bibliography

ALLPORT, G. W. (1955). *Becoming*. New Haven, Conn.: Yale University Press.
Arusha Declaration, The, and Tanu's Policy on Socialism and Self-reliance (1967). Dar-es-Salaam, Publicity Section, Tanu.
BION, W. R. (1961). *Experiences in Groups and Other Papers*. London: Tavistock; New York: Basic Books.
BLACKBURN, ROBIN (1967). The Unequal Society. In R. Blackburn & A. Cockburn (1967).
—— & COCKBURN, ALEXANDER (1967). *The Incompatibles: Trade Union Militancy and the Consensus*. Harmondsworth: Penguin Books.
BLOFELD, JOHN (1965). *The Book of Change, a new translation of the ancient Chinese I Ching (Yi King) with detailed instruction for its practical use in Divination*. London: Allen & Unwin.
BROWN, NORMAN O. (1966). *Love's Body*. New York: Random House.
COMMISSION ON INTERNATIONAL DEVELOPMENT (1969). *Partners in Development* (The Pearson Report). New York: Praeger.
CURLE, ADAM (1971). *Making Peace*. London: Tavistock.
DOLCI, DANILO (1961). *Report from Palermo*. New York: Hillman Books.
DUMONT, RENÉ (1966). *False Start in Africa*. London: Sphere Books.
ERIKSON, ERIK H. (1968). *Identity, Youth and Crisis*. New York: Norton; London: Faber.
—— (1969). *Gandhi's Truth: On the Origins of Militant Nonviolence*. New York: Norton; London: Faber, 1970.
EVANS-WENTZ, W. Y. (ed.) (1954). *The Tibetan Book of the Great Liberation, or The Method of Realizing Nirvana through Knowing the Mind*, with a commentary by C. G. Jung. London: Oxford University Press.
FAIRBAIRN, W. R. D. (1952). *Psychoanalytic Studies of the Personality*. London: Tavistock/Routledge. Also published under the title *Object-relations Theory of the Personality*. New York: Basic Books, 1954.
FANON, FRANTZ (1967). *Toward the African Revolution*. New York and London: Monthly Review Press.

BIBLIOGRAPHY

FRANK, JEROME D. (1968). *Sanity and Survival: Psychological Aspects of War and Peace.* New York: Random House.

FREUD, ERNST (ed.) (1960). *Letters of Sigmund Freud.* New York: Basic Books; London: Hogarth, 1961.

FREUD, SIGMUND (1901). *The Psychopathology of Everyday Life.* Standard Edition, Vol. 6. London: Hogarth.

FROMM, ERICH (1956). *The Art of Loving.* New York: Harper; London: Allen & Unwin, 1957.

GALTUNG, JOHAN (1969a). Peace, Peace-Theory, and an International Peace Academy. International Peace Research Institute, Oslo, International Peace Research Association, Groningen, and Gandhian Institute of Studies, Varanasi. PRIO Publications No. 23-8, Varanasi, February. (Mimeo.)

—— (1969b). Feudalism, Structural Violence, and the Structural Theory of Violence. Paper prepared for the Third General Conference of the International Peace Research Association, Karlovy Vary, September. (Mimeo.)

GANDHI, M. K. (1927). *An Autobiography or the Story of my Experiments with Truth.* Ahmedabad: Navajivan.

GLUECK, SHELDON & GLUECK, ELEANOR (1959). *Predicting Delinquency and Crime.* Cambridge, Mass.: Harvard University Press.

GOUGH, KATHLEEN (1967). World Revolution and the Science of Man. In T. Roszak (ed.), *The Dissenting Academy.* New York: Random House; Harmondsworth: Penguin Books, 1969.

GUEVARA, CHE (1967). *Che Guevara Speaks,* edited by George Lavan. Beverly Hills, Calif.: Merit Publishers.

GURDJIEFF, G. I. (1963). *Meetings with Remarkable Men.* New York: Dutton.

HUXLEY, ALDOUS (1954). *The Doors of Perception.* London: Chatto & Windus; New York: Harper. Reissued with *Heaven and Hell* in 1959, London: Chatto; Harmondsworth: Penguin Books; New York: Harper.

—— (1956). *Heaven and Hell.* London: Chatto & Windus; New York: Harper. Reissued with *The Doors of Perception* in 1959 – see above entry.

JALÉE, PIERRE (1968). *The Pillage of the Third World.* New York and London: Monthly Review Press.

JAMES, W. (1902). *Varieties of Religious Experience.* London.

JUNG, C. G. (1961). *Memories, Dreams, Reflections.* New York: Pantheon; London: Routledge/Collins, 1963.

BIBLIOGRAPHY

KING, CORETTA (1969). *My Life with Martin Luther King.* New York: Holt, Rinehart & Winston; London: Hodder & Stoughton, 1970.

KLEIN, MELANIE (1932). *The Psycho-analysis of Children.* London: Hogarth. Later editions, London: Hogarth, 1959; New York: Hillary House, 1963.

LAING, R. D. (1960). *The Divided Self.* London: Tavistock. Reprinted 1969, London: Tavistock; New York: Pantheon.

—— (1967). *The Politics of Experience.* Harmondsworth: Penguin Books; New York: Pantheon.

LAKEY, GEORGE (1969). Strategy for Non-violent Revolution. *Peace News*, 12 December.

LALL, ARTHUR (1966). *Modern International Negotiation: Principles and Practice.* New York: Columbia University Press.

LEARY, TIMOTHY F. (1968). *High Priest.* New York: New American Library.

LOGAN, A. (1970). Around City Hall. *New Yorker*, 6 June.

LUTHULI, ALBERT (1962). *Let My People Go: An Autobiography.* London: Collins.

MASLOW, ABRAHAM H. (1968). *Toward a Psychology of Being.* Second edition. Princeton, N.J.: Van Nostrand.

MORRIS, BEN (1966). The Contribution of Psychology to the Study of Education. In J. W. Tibble (ed.), *The Study of Education.* London: Routledge.

—— (1972). *Objectives and Perspectives in Education.* London: Routledge.

MYRDAL, GUNNAR (1944). *An American Dilemma.* New York and London: Harper.

NATIONAL ADVISORY COMMISSION ON CIVIL DISORDERS (1968). *Report.* New York: Bantam Books.

NYERERE, JULIUS (1967). *Freedom and Unity: A Selection from Writings and Speeches 1952–1965.* London: Oxford University Press.

—— (1968). *Ujamaa: Essays on Socialism.* Dar es Salaam: Oxford University Press (Eastern Africa).

OUSPENSKY, P. D. (1949). *In Search of the Miraculous.* New York: Harcourt, Brace & World; London: Routledge, 1950.

PATON, ALAN (1944). *Cry, the Beloved Country.* London: Cape.

PIRE, DOMINIQUE (1967). *Building Peace.* London: Corgi Books.

REICH, CHARLES (1970). *The Greening of America.* New York: Random House; London: Allen Lane, 1971.

ROSZAK, THEODORE (ed.) (1967). *The Dissenting Academy.* New York: Random House; Harmondsworth: Penguin Books, 1969.

SCHACHTEL, E. G. (1959). *Metamorphosis: on the Development of Affect, Perception, Attention and Memory*. New York: Basic Books.
SCHUTZ, WILLIAM C. (1967). *Joy: Expanding Human Awareness*. New York: Grove Press.
SUZUKI, D. T. (1960). *Manual of Zen Buddhism*. New York: Grove Press.
SZASZ, THOMAS (1965). *The Ethics of Psychoanalysis: The Theory and Method of Autonomous Psychotherapy*. New York: Basic Books.
TITMUSS, R. M. (1962). *Income Distribution and Social Change*. London: Allen & Unwin.
TRIST, E. L. & BAMFORTH, K. W. (1951). Some Social and Psychological Consequences of the Longwall Method of Coal-getting. *Human Relations* **4** (1).
US DEPARTMENT OF HEALTH, EDUCATION AND WELFARE (1969). *Toward a Social Report*. Washington, D.C.: US Government Printing Office.
WORSLEY, PETER (1967). *The Third World*. London: Weidenfeld & Nicolson.

Name Index

Bion, W. R., 12, 97
Blackburn, R., 5
Blofeld, J., 69
Brown, N. O., 12

Castro, Fidel, 55
Churchill, Sir Winston, 43, 87
Cockburn, A., 5
Curle, A., 1

Dolci, D., 88
Dumont, R., 110

Erikson, E. H., 11, 12, 26, 27–8, 87
Evans-Wentz, W. Y., 12, 111

Fairbairn, W. R. D., 12
Fanon, F., 87
Freud, S., 12, 22, 23, 27–8, 47, 84, 92
Fromm, E., 12

Galtung, J., 110
Gandhi, M. K., 10, 17, 23, 87
Glueck, E., 37, 111
Glueck, S., 37, 111
Gough, K., 110
Guevara, Che, 56, 57, 111
Gurdjieff, G. I., 12, 22, 69

Huxley, A., 64

Jalée, P., 4
James, W., 111
Jung, C. G., 22, 47, 55, 84

Khan, A. H., 88
King, Coretta, 111
King, Martin Luther, 88
Klein, M., 12

Laing, R. D., 12
Lakey, G., 57, 111
Leary, T., 65, 87
Logan, A., 111
Luthuli, A., 88

Maslow, A. H., 12, 85
Morris, B., 12
Myrdal, G., 110

Nyerere, J., 87, 110

Ouspensky, P. D., 12, 22, 69

Pascal, B., 17, 111
Paton, A., 87, 111
Piaget, J., 47
Pire, D., 55, 111
Pope John XXIII, 88

Reich, C., 111
Rigby, A., 68, 111
Roszak, T., 7, 67
Russell, Bertrand, 54

Schutz, W. C., 111
Suzuki, D. T., 12
Szasz, T., 111

Titmuss, R. M., 5
Trist, E. L., 12

Subject Index

adjustment, 37, 44
America, 5, 8, 11
   black population, 2, 58, 88, 102, 110
   construction workers, 50, 104
   Harvard University, 11
art, and perception, 16, 20, 22
autonomy, 5, 14, 15, 16, 54, 66, 67, 70, 78, 85, 94, 95
awareness, 10, 12, 13–25, 27, 34, 36, 66, 98, 100–1, 103, 108
   awakening of, 70, 101
   centre of gravity of, 16, 17, 22, 35
   change in levels of, 16, 52–4, 92–102
   counterfeit (false) high awareness, 19, 36, 63–4, 72, 79, 86, 104
   growth of, 3, 4, 21
   higher, 9, 35, 44, 54–91, 92, 95, 104, 105, 107
   lower, 9, 13–16, 34–5, 41, 48, 49, 53, 56, 57, 63, 79, 92, 95, 99, 104, 105
   natural, 10, 17–18, 19, 20, 22, 23, 33, 54–62, 63, 83–4
   and negative emotions, 16, 89, 92–4
   and (ir)rationality, 9, 13
   self-conscious, 10, 18–19, 20, 22, 23, 35, 36, 54–62, 83, 96, 97
   and spontaneity, 15
   supraliminal, 10, 19–22, 23, 35, 36, 47, 54, 55, 62–83, 84, 91, 97
   as a threat, 42, 108–9
   see also configurations of awareness and identity
awareness-identity, 9, 26, 28, 29, 31–3, 34–5, 44, 49, 53, 54, 80, 83, 87, 90, 95, 104, 105, 106, 108
   and age, 105–6, 107

Bangladesh, 88
bargaining, 3, 6, 106, 107
belonging-identity, 6, 9, 10, 12, 26, 27–31, 32, 33, 34–5, 41–9, 53, 54, 55, 56, 63, 67, 71, 72, 84, 86, 92, 93, 95, 97, 98, 104, 105, 108
black races,
   in America, 2, 58, 102, 110
   in South Africa, 5
Britain, 5, 11, 110

case studies
   type 1, 37–41
   type 2, 49–51
   type 3a, 58–62
   type 3b, 72–83
   type 4, 87–90
   see configurations of awareness and identity
charisma, 43
collaboration, 1, 3
communes, 64, 67, 68, 69, 70, 103
competitive materialism, 6–8, 20, 30, 35, 37, 48, 49, 52, 92, 97, 103
conciliation, 3, 6, 106, 107
configurations of awareness and identity
   type 1, 34, 36–41, 104
   type 2, 35, 41–51, 104
   type 3a, 35, 54–62, 104
   type 3b, 35, 62–83, 104
   type 4, 35, 83–91

SUBJECT INDEX

conflict, 1, 2, 3, 8, 24
confrontation, 3, 11, 103, 105
conservatism, 9, 26, 29, 30, 43–4
counter-culture, 20, 36, 64, 67–9, 75–6, 103
   as a threat, 67, 68
counterfeit (false) high awareness, 19, 36, 63–4, 72, 79, 86, 104
crime, 36, 37–8, 105

development, 3, 7, 11, 106, 107
drugs, 16, 20, 21, 64–7, 74–5, 81, 82, 83

education, 3, 103
equality/inequality, 3, 6, 29, 49, 103, 104, 107
Esalen Institute, 97
establishment, 42, 68
evolution, 55, 106
exploitative network, 4–6, 8, 35, 36, 48, 49, 52, 56, 103

France, 103, 110

Guinea, 110

hippies, 10, 64, 68, 72, 79–80, 84

identity, 11, 14, 26–33, 34, 36, 41, 53, 54, 57
   see also awareness-identity; belonging-identity; configurations of awareness and identity
India, 5, 88
insight, 9, 10, 12, 16, 22, 52, 56, 82, 84, 93
introjection, 48

justice/injustice, 3, 4, 6, 29, 103

Latin America, 5, 11, 60
law and order, 105

loving relationships, 46, 71

manipulation of others, 18, 46
mask, 32, 33, 52
mask–mirage function, 12, 23–5, 26, 34–5, 47, 56
mediation, 6, 107
militants, 10, 11, 12, 23, 26, 36, 49, 50, 54, 57–8, 59, 63, 64, 67, 68, 72–4, 80, 83, 84, 90, 91, 95, 103–4
moral beliefs, 16, 18, 85
mystics, 10, 11, 12, 21, 23, 26, 36, 49, 50, 63, 67, 80, 83, 90, 95, 103–4

negative emotions, and awareness, 16, 89, 92–4
nirvana, 20, 64, 70–2, 78–9, 111
non-violence, 56, 57, 72, 79, 88
   see also violence

objectivity, 18

Pakistan, 5, 11, 80, 88
patriotism, 9, 29, 31, 34, 42, 48
peace, definition of, 1
peaceful relationships, 1, 108
   see also unpeacefulness relationships
peacemakers, 3–4, 105–8
peacemaking, 1–4, 103, 106, 107, 108
pollution, 8
poor nations, relationship with rich nations, 4–5
power, 111
   (im)balance of, 3, 5–6
pride, 29, 30, 93
projection, 23, 48
psychology, 11, 12, 19, 22
psycho-philosophy, 12, 64, 69–70, 76–8, 83, 100
psychotherapy, 10, 15, 16, 19, 82, 93, 96

relationship(s)
   between black and white races, 5

SUBJECT INDEX

relationship(s)—*cont.*
  between industry and military, 8
  loving, 46, 71
  between rich and poor nations, 4-5
  between slave and master, 2-3
  web of, 108
  see also peaceful relationships; unpeaceful relationships
religion(s), 12, 17, 42, 78, 85-6, 89, 90, 99-100
responsibility, 17
revolution(ary), 3, 10, 30, 43, 44, 55, 56, 57, 60, 81, 88, 103, 106
rich nations, relationship with poor nations, 4-5

self-discipline, 99
sensitivity training, 10, 19, 82, 97, 100
Sicily, 88
slave, relationship with master, 2-3, 43
South Africa, 5, 40
spontaneity, 15
stress (tension), 21, 24, 27, 53
students, 11, 56, 84, 103

Tanzania, 5, 110
Tavistock Institute of Human Relations, 12
technology, 7, 37, 49, 97, 102, 106
  compared with science, 7

and pollution, 8
T-groups, 19, 81, 82, 97, 98
Third World, 4, 7, 40, 101, 110
threat
  of awareness, 42, 108-9
  of counter-culture, 67, 68

UK, *see* Britain
USA, *see* America
unpeaceful relationships, 1-3, 5, 11, 85, 103, 107, 108, 110
  see also peaceful relationships

values, system of, 16, 18, 35, 48
  B-values, 85
Vietnam, 5, 6, 40, 59
violence, 1, 2, 5, 31, 36, 45, 46, 49, 51, 56, 57, 72, 79, 83, 92, 104, 105, 108
  and non-violence, 56, 57, 72, 79, 88
  'soft', 110
  structural, 110

war, 5, 6, 25, 46, 49
  guerrilla, 5
  between India and Pakistan, 5-6
  nuclear, 8
withdrawal, 20, 26, 71, 79, 82

zombies, 95

LIBRARY OF DAVIDSON COLLEGE

Books on regular loan may be checked out for **two weeks.** Books must be presented at the Circulation Desk in order to be renewed.

A fine is charged after date due.

Special books are subject to special regulations at the discretion of library staff.

JAN. 20, 1983

FEB. -1, 1989